Lessons on the Holy spirit

by

Elmer Moore

Preface

This work is a compilation of a series of lessons on the Holy Spirit brother Moore preached over a period of many years. Improvements were continually made on these lessons as a result of questions that were asked by brethren in the many different places he preached them.

ISBN 10: 1-58427-308-9
ISBN 13: 978-158427-308-0

Truth Books
P.O. Box 9670
Bowling Green, Kentucky 42102
1-800-428-0121
www.truthbooks.net

THE NAMES OF THE HOLY SPIRIT.

A. Names Used In Old Testament.

1. Holy Spirit. ______________________ Psa. 51:11
2. Spirit of God. ____________________ Gen. 1:2
3. Spirit of the Lord. ________________ Isa. 11:2
4. Spirit of the Lord God. ____________ Isa. 61:1
5. Good Spirit. _____________________ Neh. 9:20
6. His Spirit. ________________________ Isa. 48:16

B. Names used in the New Testament.

1. Spirit ___________________________ Mk. 1:10
2. Holy Spirit________________________ "Lk. 11:13
3. Holy Ghost _______________________ Jno. 14:26
4. Comforter_________________________ Jno. 14:26
5. Spirit of Truth_____________________ Jno. 16:13
6. Spirit of your Father________________ Mat. 10:20
7. Spirit of God_______________________ Mat. 3:16
8. Spirit of Christ _____________________ I PE. 1:11
9. Eternal Spirit_______________________ Heb. 9:14

THE HOLY SPIRIT IS A PERSON.

A. He demonstrates the actions of personhood

1. He speaks.__________________________ I Tim. 4:1
2. He testifies___________________________ Jno. 15:26
3. He witnesses_________________________ Rom. 8:16
4. He teaches___________________________ Jno. 14:26
5. He guides____________________________ Jno. 16:13
6. He hears_____________________________ Jno. 16:13
7. He shows_____________________________ Jno. 16:13
8. He forbids____________________________ Acts 16:6,7
9. He searches___________________________ I Cor. 2:10

B. <u>He possesses the qualities of personhood</u>.

1. Mind___________________________Rom. 8:27
2. Love ___________________________Rom. 15:30-32
3. Knowledge _______________________I Cor. 2:11
4. Goodness________________________Neh. 9:20
5. Will_____________________________I Cor. 12:11
6. Judgement_______________________Acts 15:38

C. <u>The things that can be done unto him demonstrate personality. He can be:</u>

1. Lied to__________________________Acts 5:3
2. Resisted_________________________Acts 7:51
3. Despised________________________Heb. 10:29
4. Blasphemed_____________________Mat. 12:31
5. Grieved__________________________Eph. 4:30
6. Vexed. __________________________Isa. 63:10

TABLE OF CONTENTS

IV. Holy Spirit and Miracles 73

V. Gift of The Spirit and Indwelling 105

CHAPTER ONE

"Basic Truths About The Holy Spirit"

I am certainly pleased that you are here and I hope that I will be able to present a lesson that will be profitable to you. I have preached on this series of lessons a number of times and in some instances, I have been told, "Well we want to ask some questions after each lesson" and I have no problem with that except that I am usually asked about something that I will present in a lesson or two later. So, I don't think you would want me to cover all of the material that I have brought with me in one lesson. So, if there are questions and if you will jot them down, I will address that in the process of the presentation. My first chart this morning will contain a list of very important questions that I will answer in this series of lessons. Today, I will talk about something that I consider to be very basic and essential in order to reach the proper conclusion about the Holy Spirit. You know, if you start off wrong you will likely end up wrong. I will talk tomorrow morning about what the bible says about Holy Spirit baptism. Tuesday morning I will talk about the Holy Spirit and the word, about inspiration. Thursday we will talk about the Holy Spirit and miracles and we will pay special attention to the speaking in tongues and then on Friday morning we will conclude the series with a dual lesson: 1) The "gift of the Holy Spirit", (Acts 2:38) and 2) the Holy Spirit indwelling the Christian. That is really two lessons but I will cover them in one.

There is a lot of confusion about the subject of the Holy Spirit, I know that all to well. I don't claim to be an authority on the subject and I don't claim to know all there is to know about it. But I believe that I know enough to keep from taking a false position on it. There are some things about God that I cannot comprehend but I can comprehend enough to keep me from taking a false position about deity. So, I admit that I recognize my limitations and yet I believe that we can learn enough about what the book teaches on this subject to avoid teaching things that are wrong. God is not responsible for the confusion that exist in the world over the subject of the Holy Spirit for "God is not the author of confusion but of peace", (I Cor. 14:34). It is not just the Charismatics that have some wrong views about the Holy Spirit; We have some brethren that hold views about the Holy Spirit that is totally foreign to what the New Testament teaches. I think that the erroneous views on this subject are responsible for some of the associated doctrines as well. So, we will do our best to study the subject.

Chart #1
QUESTIONS OF IMPORTANCE
1. Does the Holy Spirit have a mission? If so, what is it? 2. How is the word SPIRIT used in the New Testament? 3. Is the Holy Spirit a person? 4. Who were baptized in the Holy Spirit? 5. What does it mean to be filled with the Spirit? 6. How does the Spirit : lead, convict men of sin, bear witness, make elders, and indwell the Christians? 7. What part did the Spirit play in the revelation of truth? 8. Does the Spirit enable men to speak tongues & work miracles today?
What Is "Gift" Of The Holy Spirit?

Let me suggest to you that the word "spirit" occurs over 200 times in the American Standard. I have looked at all of those text. Some time ago in Lufkin, Texas I was studying with some preacher friends and I was asked to discuss all of the passages that show the term "Spirit" being used to mean an attitude or disposition. I have a notebook with all of those scriptures along with notes and I think that is the way we ought to study a subject. I don't propose to do that with you in the lesson this morning, you know that I cannot in the time frame. However, I do want you to know that it is important to take a look at what the book has to say about any subject. Thus, when it comes to what the Holy Spirit is; what the Holy Spirit does; what He does not do, He will be the one to tell us. In other words: What does the Holy Spirit say about Himself? So, the proper way to answer these questions is to let the Holy Spirit give us the answer through the word that He inspired men to speak and to record.

In Eph. 3, if you want to turn there, the Apostle Paul talked about the message, the truth. He said in verse 3 "how that by revelation He made known to me the mystery (as I wrote before in a few words, by which, when you read, you may understand my knowledge in the mystery of Christ), which in other ages was not made known to the sons of men, as it has now been revealed by the Spirit to His holy apostles and prophets:" Thus, the message I hold in my hand is the message that the Holy Spirit has revealed. Therefore, if I want to know the truth about the Holy Spirit, I will read what He says about it. That is the only place I know that I can get the proper information. In II Pet. 1:20-21, Peter says: "knowing this first, that no prophecy of Scripture is of any private interpretation, for prophecy never came by the will of man, but holy men of God spoke as they were moved by the Holy Spirit." And by that he means that man is not the one that is responsible for scripture, it did not originate in the mind of man and therefore, it is not of private interpretation. The context will help you see that verse 21 tells you what is meant by the statement in verse 20. This is quite often the case, that a writer will explain a statement in the following verse or verses, in the immediate context. It simply means that God's word did not originate in the mind of man, it is not something that man is the author of. So, it is not of man's own loosening for he said "prophecy never came by the will of man, but holy men of God spoke as they were moved by the Holy Spirit". So, we have the element of inspiration involved. So, what the Holy Spirit has to say about Himself is what I ought to believe. It is not uncommon for people to level the charge at us that we do not believe in the Holy Spirit. I have been on a number of talk shows and have people call up and say: "Well you just don't believe in the Holy Spirit". I answer, "Oh yes I do. You are the fellow that doesn't believe in the Holy Spirit". I say that because if a person doesn't believe what the Holy Spirit says about Himself, that person does not believe in the Holy Spirit. We need to put the shoe on the foot where it belongs. These people who tell you what they think about it are not interested in what the Holy Spirit says about Himself. We are interested in the truth ; we want valid information about the Holy Spirit, not just what someone thinks about it. There is a lot of invalid information, information that is not reliable, not dependable. I think you understand what I mean by subjective information. I mean something that has to do with man, what he thinks about it. It is not reliable, it is unreliable.

Chart #2 **THE HOLY SPIRIT:** **Source of valid information**
<u>SUBJECTIVE INFORMATION</u> • Unreliable : Fallible Men(cf. Jackson/Robertson) <u>OBJECTIVE INFORMATION</u> • Reliable: Inspired Source(cf. Jno. 14:26;15:26;16:12-13; Rom. 8:2) The Holy Spirit has Revealed The truth about Himself
<u>BE SATISFIED WITH HIS DESCRIPTION</u>

There are two men that stand out in contemporaneous times, and they are Jesse Jackson and Pat Robertson. Both of these men claim to be guided by and directed by the Holy Spirit. What is so interesting about these two men is that they do not believe the same thing religiously. They are part of two different religious concepts that are at odds with one another. Both of them will tell you that the Lord called them to preach and yet, the Lord called one man to preach one thing and called the other one to preach something else entirely different and even contradictory. Then, low and behold, the Lord told them to get out of preaching and get into politics. And we are to believe that He called one to get on the Democratic ticket and the other to get on the Republican ticket. That is what we are suppose to accept, that kind of information. Ladies and gentlemen that is not proper information it is not reliable.

There is objective information, it is reliable it is of an inspired source. These are passages I will be looking at from time to time in our study, the source of objective information. Jesus said, in the presence of His ambassadors, the apostles, that the Holy Spirit would come and would guide them in all truth, teach them all things, bring to their remembrance all that he had said to them and declare unto them things to come; He would also validate their message and that is what the passages we will look at teach. So, I have valid information.

The Lord said, that the Holy Spirit would come and guide them into all truth and validate them and their message. That message is called the Spirit's Law, In Rom. 8:2, Paul said: "For the law of the Spirit of life in Christ Jesus has made me free from the law of sin and death." The Law of the Spirit produces life and we are interested in that Law, the Spirit's Law. The Holy Spirit has revealed the truth about Himself and I had better be satisfied with that description.

Chart #3
THINGS THE HOLY SPIRIT WILL NOT DO
The Holy Spirit Will Not Guide: (I Cor. 14:33) * Men to teach conflicting Doctrines * Men to teach Doctrines contrary to the word of God * Men to perform acts contrary to, or different from the word of God
Don't Blame or Credit Him , He is not responsible

There are some things, that I guarantee you, the Holy Spirit is not going to do because He is not the author of confusion but of peace. The Holy Spirit is not going to guide men to teach conflicting doctrine. Can you imagine that He would. The Holy Spirit is said to be divine and we will talk about that more in a little bit. So, here you have the Holy Spirit, God, directing one man to teach one thing and another man to teach something that is in conflict one with the other while all the time the scriptures tell us that He is not the author of confusion but of peace. He is not going to do that. He is not going to guide men to do that and He is not going to guide men to teach doctrines contrary to the Word of God because this is the message that He inspired the apostles to uncover and record. So, He is not going to guide men to teach things contrary to what He has revealed. Not only is that the case, He is not going to guide men to perform acts, elements of worship, contrary to or different from the Word of God. You do not blame the Holy Spirit or credit Him as being the author of these conflicting concepts because He is not responsible for all of that.

I have heard it told, and I partly believe it, of a fellow who had just got into town for a meeting and he apologized and said "I didn't have time to get ready for this so I will just let the Holy Spirit lay it on my heart and tomorrow night I'll try to do better" . I think there is an element of truth in that. They know they are going to make a mess of it so they want to blame somebody else for it. But you can't blame or credit the Holy Spirit for what these fellows teach.

Chart #4
THE HOLY SPIRIT IS A PERSON
DEFINITION: "PERSON" "In Theology, a term applied to each of the three beings of the Godhead" (Web. Unabrd.) DEFINITION: "BEING" 1) "Existence as opposed to nonexistence: that which exists in any form, whether actual or ideal" (Webster) 2) "Conscious existence" (Am. Col, Encyl. Dict.) BASIC IDEA: AN INDIVIDUAL WITH CONSCIOUS EXISTENCE
IF NOT A PERSON THEN NON-EXISTENT

The word "Ghost" used in the King James Version has left a wrong impression in the minds of some. This is not a matter of kicking the King James. It is not that at all because at the time it was translated, the word "Ghost" meant the same thing as the word "Spirit" means now. Many people think of the Holy Spirit as an "it" or some kind of gas or vapor and that comes from the word "Ghost". I think that is where the problem is in the misunderstanding of Holy Spirit. The United Pentecostals are very outspoken in their belief and they deny that the Holy Spirit is a person. They go to Luke 24:39 where Jesus said "A Spirit has not flesh and bones as you see me have" and they argue that for the Holy Spirit to be a person He would have to have flesh and bones, and since He doesn't have flesh and bones He is not a person. That is exactly how they argue. I know this because I have met them in debate at least four times. What they do is to look at a fleshly human being and say that he is a person. Therefore, they say a person has to be a fleshly human being. That does not follow. That is like looking at a cow and saying a cow is an animal and therefore an animal is a cow. That just does not follow. Admittedly, a fleshly human being is a person but a person does not demand that one be a fleshly human being. A person simply means that one exists (By existence is meant that which exist permanently, not as the lower animals , birds, plants and etc. that exists only temporarily. For instance, Abraham and Isaac exist although they have been physically dead for centuries.) and they absolutely deny the existence of the Holy Spirit and do not realize that they do. They do it by their concept of what a person is.

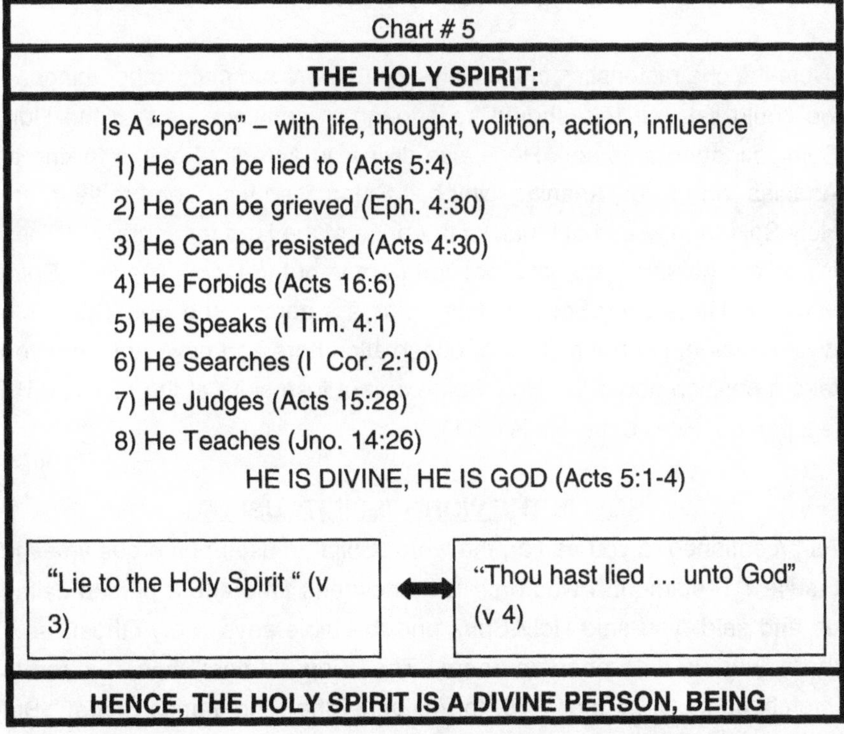

Chart # 5

THE HOLY SPIRIT:

Is A "person" – with life, thought, volition, action, influence

1) He Can be lied to (Acts 5:4)
2) He Can be grieved (Eph. 4:30)
3) He Can be resisted (Acts 4:30)
4) He Forbids (Acts 16:6)
5) He Speaks (I Tim. 4:1)
6) He Searches (I Cor. 2:10)
7) He Judges (Acts 15:28)
8) He Teaches (Jno. 14:26)

HE IS DIVINE, HE IS GOD (Acts 5:1-4)

"Lie to the Holy Spirit " (v 3) ⟷ "Thou hast lied ... unto God" (v 4)

HENCE, THE HOLY SPIRIT IS A DIVINE PERSON, BEING

The Holy Spirit is a person, there is not any question about that. The term person is defined as follows: "In Theology, a term applied to each of the three <u>beings</u> of the Godhead" ,(Webster Unabridged). In case you are not aware of it, the unabridged section of Webster's Dictionary goes back to the etymology of the word, the root meaning of it. I recommend that you use it when you are trying to understand the meaning of a word, especially biblical terms. The word "being" which occurs in that definition also means "existence as opposed to non-existence; that which exists in any form, whether actual or ideal" (Webster) . The American College Encyclopaedia Dictionary says it is "conscious existence" . A word is a symbol of an idea and a person is one with a conscious existence. So, I submit to you that the Holy Spirit is in fact a person and to deny that the Holy Spirit is a person is to deny that the Holy Spirit exists. I believe this is one of those consequences that have been pointed out to those people who deny that the Holy Spirit is a person, they deny that He exists; they don't know it but they are, in reality. So, the basic idea is that a person is an individual with conscious existence. The bible uses such language that demands that I recognize that the Holy Spirit is a person with life, thought, volition, action and influence.

Note the cha racteristics of the Holy Spirit. There are many other things we could list, but this should be enough to convince us that the Holy Spirit is indeed a person. He is also divine. In Acts 5:3,Peter is talking to Ananias and said: "Ananias, why has Satan filled your heart to lie to the Holy Spirit and keep back part of the price of the land for yourself?" Then in verse 4 he said "you have not lied to men but to God." The Holy Spirit is divine, He is God. So, the Holy Spirit is a person, the Holy Spirit is a divine person. Let me make this observation here and now. Any time you take a position about the Holy Spirit, do not lose sight of the fact that He is a person, He is deity, He is God.

HOW IS THE WORD "SPIRIT" USED?

As I mentioned to you earlier, the word "Spirit" is used numerous times in the New Testament. I was on a talk show one time and a person called up and said "you said Holy Spirit and the bible says "Holy Ghost" as if there was a difference in them. The King James uses the terms interchangeably. In Jno. 7:39, for instance, the King James reads: "(But this spake he of the Spirit, which they that believe on him should receive: for the Holy Ghost was not yet given; because that Jesus was not yet glorified.)" The terms are used interchangeably and the same thing is true in Acts 2:4; "And they were all filled with the Holy Ghost, and began to speak with other tongues, as the Spirit gave them utterance." So, the King James uses them interchangeably, there is no difference at all. These are the people who claim to be inspired, these are the people who claim to be guided by the Holy Spirit and yet, they are not aware of the fact that the terms "Holy Spirit" and "Holy Ghost" are terms that mean the same thing, that refer to that one divine being.

Chart #6
HOW IS THE WORD "SPIRIT" USED?
HUMAN (Jam. 2:26) ATTITUDE 1) Spirit of Bondage/Adoption (Rom. 8:15) 2) Spirit of Stupor / Slumber (Rom. 11:8) 3) Spirit of Antichrist (1 Jno. 4:3) 4) Spirit of Truth (1 Jno. 4:6) 5) Spirit of Gentleness / Meekness (Gal. 6:1) 6) Spirit of Wisdom (Ex. 28:3) **HOLY SPIRIT** (Jno. 14:26) 1) Miraculous Effect (Heb. 2:4) 2) Holy Spirit Baptism (Acts 2:1-4) 3) Cause for Effect (Bullinger, Figures of Speech, P540) **NOTE:** The context & related passages will have to be the deciding factor The Author for His Writings (Acts 8:28; 15:21; Eph 4:21) The Holy Spirit for His Law (Rom. 8:2; Jno. 3:6; I Pet. 1:22) **"SPIRIT" = Human, Attitude, Holy Spirit**

I want to tell you about a card that I received in the mail from a fellow that didn't like what I had been saying on my Radio Broadcast. This was a card, mind you, that anyone could read and he said that I was ignorant and he didn't spell the word correctly . He said that I didn't have the "hely gust" and if I knew the "lard" I would know better. I do not mention this to belittle the man because he couldn't spell simple words but to point out that anytime a man claims to be guided by the Holy Spirit and doesn't even know how to spell the term it is a sad commentary. Can you imagine what people, who didn't believe the bible, thought when they read that? But there is the idea that there is a difference in the Holy Ghost and the Holy Spirit in their minds. Many, if not all, of the modern translations of the bible uses the term "Holy Spirit" consistently throughout. I know that the American Standard does and the word "Spirit' or "spirit" appears 246 times, by my count.

How Is The Word "Spirit" Used?

Men will open their bible and see the word "Spirit" and immediately conclude that it is the Holy Spirit. Some do not stop there but conclude that it is some miraculous effect or Holy Spirit baptism. I know that is what happens and many of our brethren will do that too. They pay no attention as to how the word is being use. Let me point out that the capital "S" does not necessarily mean that it is the Holy Spirit, it only means that those who published that version thought that it did. That is a thumb rule. One of the things about a "thumb rule" is that there are exceptions to it. So, you don't determine that by whether it is capitalized or not. You must look at the context. Note, if you will, that the term "spirit" sometimes has reference to the human spirit . In Jam. 2:26, James said "the body without the spirit is dead". So, when I see the word "spirit" I need to find out if it is talking about the soul of man. I know that the words "spirit" and "soul" are used interchangeably. So, sometimes it is used to refer to the human spirit. Many times it is used to refer to an attitude. We sometimes talk about somebody manifesting a bad spirit. What do we mean? We mean that his attitude is bad. It is used in the bible in just that same way. In Rom. 8:15, Paul said: "For you did not receive the spirit of bondage again to fear, but you received the Spirit of adoption by whom we cry out, "Abba, Father." Now then, is the spirit of bondage the Holy Spirit? And again, Paul says, in Rom. 11:8: "Just as it is written: 'God has given them a spirit of stupor, eyes that they should not see and ears that they should not hear, to this very day'." Is this "spirit of stupor" talking about the Holy Spirit? No it is not.

Then in I Jno 4:3, John is writing about the spirit of Antichrist. Holy Spirit, no he is talking about the disposition of one who is opposed to Christ. And in verse 6 he talks about the spirit of truth and the spirit of error; talking about an attitude toward truth, advancing truth, teaching truth as opposed to the spirit or error. Again, in Gal. 6:1, Paul says; "Brethren, if a man is overtaken in any trespass, you who are spiritual restore such a one in a spirit of gentleness, considering yourself lest you also be tempted." Is this "spirit of gentleness", talking about the Holy Spirit? No, it is talking about an attitude. So, many times the bible uses the word "spirit" to refer to an attitude.

Sometimes the word "Spirit" is used to refer to the Holy Spirit, I know that. In Heb. 2:4 we read: "God also bearing witness both with signs and wonders, with various miracles, and gifts of the Holy Spirit, according to His own will?" There is no question that the writer is talking about some miraculous effect. In Acts the Second Chapter, I believe I can show that the passage is talking about Holy Spirit baptism when they were filled with the Spirit and they began to speak as the Spirit gave them utterance. So, I believe that has reference to Holy Spirit baptism.

Sometimes, the word "Spirit" is named as the cause for its effect and that is taken from (Bullinger, Figures of Speech, p540). He is recognized as one of the leading authorities on the figures of speech in the world. He said: sometimes the 'Spirit' is named, the cause for the effect. That is, the author for his writing. So, that is a figure of speech we need to recognize and that it is not uncommon for the author to be named when his law or writing is intended. If I ask you, "Have you read Shakespeare?" you know what I am asking you. I am asking if you have read the writings of Shakespeare. In Acts 8:28, the record says the Ethiopian Eunuch was reading Isaiah the Prophet. Was he reading the prophet's mind? No, he was reading what the prophet wrote. Other similar passages are Acts 15:21 and Eph. 4:21.

The Holy Spirit For His Law

Likewise, the passages in Rom. 8:2; Jno. 3:6 and I Pet. 1:22 illustrate the use of the word "Spirit" when His law is intended.

The Apostle Paul said, in Rom. 8:2: "For the law of the Spirit of life in Christ Jesus has made me free from the law of sin and death." The Apostle John said, in Jno. 3:6: "That which is born of the flesh is flesh, and that which is born of the Spirit is spirit." The Apostle Peter said, in I Pet. 1:22-23: "Since you have purified your souls in obeying the truth through the Spirit in sincere love of the brethren, love one another fervently with a pure heart, having been born again, not of corruptible seed but incorruptible, through the word of God which lives and abides forever,". So, we are born of the Spirit but begotten by the word of truth, begotten by the gospel, (I Cor. 4:15 and Jam. 1:18). So, you have been born of the Spirit but born of the truth, the Spirit is named for the Spirit's Law. Thus, in Jno. 3 where the record says " except one be born of the water and the Spirit" , water is named when water baptism is intended and the Spirit is named when the Spirit's Law is intended. Thus, when a man, according to the Spirit's Law, is baptized into Christ he is born of the water and the Spirit. If I preached an hour that is exactly the conclusion I would reach. So, the Spirit is named when the Spirit's Law is intended. Thus, "Spirit" sometimes has reference to the human spirit; sometimes has reference to an attitude; sometimes has reference to the Spirit's Law; sometimes has reference to the Holy Spirit; and sometimes to Holy Spirit baptism.

How do we determine the meaning of the word "Spirit". Well we determine it by the context and I want to look at some particular passages to make that point. The following passage in Gal. 4 has been used and continues to be used as a basis for the concept of the personal indwelling of the Holy Spirit. Some of our brethren base their whole concept of the personal indwelling on this passage, I know that is the case with Roy Deaver and Mack Deaver. Mack used it in a debate that I have and Roy wrote it in an article that I have read. I have known these men for years and it is difficult for me to see how men with their intelligence, fail to see how they are perverting that passage. So, let's read the passage and then we will discuss it: So, he says: "And because you are sons, God has sent forth the Spirit of His Son into your hearts, crying out, Abba, Father!" and some say that is the Holy Spirit. How did they determine that to be the Holy Spirit? I have granted that conclusion, in debates, for the sake of argument.

Chart #7
Galatians 4:1-7 "Now I say that the heir, as long as he is a child, does not differ at all from a slave, though he is master of all, but is under guardians and stewards until the time appointed by the father. Even so we, when we were children, were in bondage under the elements of the world. But when the fullness of the time had come, God sent forth His Son, born of a woman, born under the law, to redeem those who were under the law, that we might receive the adoption as sons. And because you are sons, God has sent forth the Spirit of His Son into your hearts, crying out, "Abba, Father!" Therefore you are no longer a slave but a son, and if a son, then an heir of God through Christ."
"God has sent forth the Spirit of His Son"

I granted it for a reason because the Oneness Pentecost argue that the New Birth involves water baptism and Holy Spirit baptism. They argue that one must have Holy Spirit baptism in order to be born again and they cite this passage. I say to them, "that does not fit your theory friend. Your theory is that you must have Holy Spirit baptism and water baptism in order to be born again and in order to become a son of God and you quote a passage that says because you are sons of God ". So, I grant the contention in order to point out their inconsistency on that. They say it is to make them sons and that passages says because you are sons, not in order that you might become sons. Now, is that talking about the Holy Spirit? Let's take a look. The writer is talking about the law and their attitude under that law and uses this simple illustration about this heir that is under tutors until the time appointed by the Father.

So, he says, even so we when we were children were in bondage of the elements of the world. "But when the fullness of the time had come, God sent forth His Son, born of a woman, born under the law, to redeem those who were under the law, that we might receive the adoption as sons. And because you are sons, God has sent forth the Spirit of His Son". This is talking about the disposition or attitude of sonship. To put the Holy Spirit in that passage is to violate ever basic rule of biblical hermeneutics that has every been known. It is not talking about the Holy

Spirit, it is talking about an attitude or disposition. So, you are sons now and you serve God because you are sons and God has put forth the spirit of His son in your heart.

Now look at Rom. 8 and tell me Paul is not talking about the same thing.

Chart #8
Romans 8:14-17 For as many as are led by the Spirit of God, these are sons of God. For ye received not the spirit of bondage again unto fear; but ye received the spirit of adoption, whereby we cry, Abba, Father. The Spirit himself beareth witness with our spirit, that we are children of God: and if children, then heirs; heirs of God, and joint-heirs with Christ; if so be that we suffer with {him}, that we may be also glorified with {him}.
You Received The Spirit of Adoption

This passage says the same thing. Paul says you serve God, not as a slave but as an adopted son. Thus, the attitude or disposition of sonship. That is what Paul wrote to the Galatians and that is what he writes here to the Romans. So, The word spirit is being use in the sense of an attitude or disposition. Did you notice in the Galatians letter how the translators capitalized "S" in the word spirit? They thought it was the Holy Spirit and some have picked up on that and said "Look there the word is spelled with a capital "S" . That does not mean a thing on earth but that the publishers or translators thought it ought to be a capital "S". There is nothing in the original Greek text to indicate it ought to be capitalized. So, the passage is used, misused and perverted; it is not talking about the Holy Spirit but about an attitude and when you look closely at the text you can see that is the case. We find in First John another text that is misused and perverted. It is just another text that deals with attitude that some insist is the Holy Spirit Himself.

"INDWELLING" IN CONTEXT

This is another passage that is used to show that God gives us the Holy Spirit and then assumes that He is in our body. This text says that God so loved us, we ought to also love one another. The kind of love God has is a love directed at some object and acts toward that object in a beneficial manner. Love must have an object; you cannot love without loving something. So, he said if God so loved us, we also should love one another, i.e . have a beneficial love for one another. Then the Apostle John concludes that "If we love one another the way God loves us, God abides in us, and His love has been perfected in us."

Chart #9
"INDWELLING" IN CONTEXT
I Jno. 4:10-17 "In this is love, not that we loved God, but that He loved us and sent His Son to be the propitiation for our sins. Beloved, if God so loved us, we also ought to love one another. No one has seen God at any time. If we love one another, God abides in us, and His love has been perfected in us. By this we know that we abide in Him, and He in us, because He has given us of His Spirit. And we have seen and testify that the Father has sent the Son as Savior of the world. Whoever confesses that Jesus is the Son of God, God abides in him, and he in God. And we have known and believed the love that God has for us. God is love, and he who abides in love abides in God, and God in him. Love has been perfected among us in this: that we may have boldness in the day of judgment; because as He is, so are we in this world."
"AS HE IS, SO ARE WE"

On This Matter Of Love

Do you remember in our Lord's sermon on the mount in Matthew Five, a text that has caused some problems through the years. Starting in verse 43 Jesus said: "You have heard that it was said, 'You shall love your neighbor and hate your enemy.' But I say to you, love your enemies, bless those who curse you, do good to those who hate you, and pray for those who spitefully use you and persecute you, that you may be sons of your Father in heaven; for He makes His sun rise on the evil and on the good, and sends rain on the just and on the unjust. For if you love those who love you, what reward have you? Do not even the tax collectors do the same? And if you greet your brethren only, what do you do more than others? Do not even the tax collectors do so? Then he said in verse 48: "Therefore you shall be perfect, just as your Father in heaven is perfect." The word perfect in this passage simply means complete, it does not mean sinless perfection as some contend. But where did they get the idea that it means sinless, where did that come from? They seem to just pluck it out of the air. Yes, I will admit that sinlessness describes a perfect condition but that is not necessarily what the word perfect means. The word perfect means complete and it is used time and time again in the New Testament in just that way. So, Jesus said you will be complete as your Father is complete. Complete in all things? No, he is talking about love, that is the subject and so He said you ought to have the kind of love God has, have a complete love like your Father's love. The kind of love God has is the kind of love that acts in a beneficial way toward some object. So, we should not hate our enemies, we should act in a beneficial way toward one another, even our enemies.

Now let's continue to read in our text in Jno. 4. John said: "because He gave us of His Spirit." Is that talking about the Holy Spirit dwelling in us? No, it is talking about an attitude, the same attitude that God has in His love for us. <u>God is love</u>, and he who abides in love abides in God, and <u>God in him</u>. This is the way love is made perfect, that we abide in God's love. In other words we have fellowship one with the other and act in a beneficial way toward one another. That is how God loves and that is how we abide in Him, by having the same kind of love He has. That is talking about a disposition of love. We must have that same disposition of love and if we do, His love is made perfect in us. Those who look at this and think Holy Spirit just look at that word "Spirit" and pay no attention to what the passage is talking about.

The passage is talking about the Spirit of God all right but it is the "Spirit" of love, not the Holy Spirit. That is the problem, ladies and gentlemen, a failure to consider the context to determine what is intended by the writer of the text. They go stone blind when they see the word "Spirit" and conclude that it is talking about the Holy Spirit or some miraculous effect of the Holy Spirit. So, I submit to you that this is talking about an attitude of love because he says: if we love as He loves then as He is so are we, we must manifest that same kind of love. There are many other passages that illustrate the meaning of the word "Spirit" to be other than the Holy Spirit or some miraculous effect of the Holy Spirit.

Chart #10
THE SPIRIT AND THE WORD **Author For His Writings**
1. "David said by the Holy Spirit," Mk. 12:36. Referring to what was WRITTEN, Psa 110:1 2. Holy Spirit said..." Heb. 3:7. Referring to what was WRITTEN, Psa 95:7-11 3. "Spirit SAYS to the churches..." Rev. 2:7,11,17,29; 3:6,13,22. 4. Resist the Holy Spirit, Acts 7:51-53, by resisting what the prophets SPOKE and WROTE. 5. Receive the promise of the Spirit, Acts 2:33, referring to what was WRITTEN in Psa 132:11
NOTE: Jno 3:3-5; I Pet. 1:22,23

Again, if we looked at all of the passages where the Spirit is named and His law is intended, we would be here for many hours. I will concentrate on a few of them instead. In Mk. 12:36, the record says: **"For David himself said by the Holy Spirit: 'The Lord said to my Lord, "Sit at My right hand, till I make Your enemies Your footstool."** ' While I am thinking about it and because I may not get to it in any of the other lessons, I want to take time to talk about the terms "By the Holy Spirit" and "Through the Holy Spirit" . In I Cor. 12, Paul talks about these terms. He writes about the different gifts of the Spirit and beginning in verse 8 he says: **"For to one is given through the Spirit the word of wisdom; and to another the word of knowledge, according to the same Spirit: to another faith, in the same Spirit; and to another gifts of healings, in the one Spirit; and to another workings of miracles; and to another prophecy; and to another discernings of spirits; to another {divers} kinds of tongues; and to another the interpretation of tongues: but all these worketh the one and the same Spirit, dividing**

to each one severally even as he will." Note that he says to one is given wisdom **<u>through</u>** the Spirit; to another knowledge **<u>according</u> <u>to</u> the same Spirit** and to another faith **<u>in</u> the same Spirit**. From this we can see that we do not have to go to the Greek in order to define "in" or "by" they both mean through or according to the Spirit; according to the directions of the Holy Spirit. It is there just as plain as day. So, "in the Spirit" ,in this text, means according to the Holy Spirit; according to the Holy Spirit's will. Where does He express His will? He expresses His will in the New Testament. Now let's go on with our lesson.

The Spirit is named when actually His word or will is intended. In hermeneutics it is, "the author for his writings". So, Mark in quoting Psa. 110:1 writes, "David said by the Holy Spirit" and we now see that this means that David <u>wrote</u> it but the Holy Spirit <u>said</u> it. In Heb. 3:7 we read, "The Holy Spirit said..." again referring to what was written by David this time in Psa. 95. The record says the Holy Spirit <u>said</u> it but it quotes that which David <u>wrote</u>. Have you ever noticed that passage in the book of Rev. 2:7 where Jesus is speaking and says: "He who has an ear, let him hear what the <u>Spirit says</u> to the churches. To him who overcomes I will give to eat from the tree of life, which is in the midst of the Paradise of God." ' It says the Spirit <u>says</u> to the churches but it was John doing the <u>writing</u>. Now, tell me that the Spirit is not named when it is the Spirit's message that is intended. This same phraseology is used several times in the second and third chapters of Revelation.

In Acts 7:51-53 we find an interesting passage where Steven is talking to the Jews that were refuting the message of the gospel. He said: **"You stiffnecked and uncircumcised in heart and ears! You always resist the Holy Spirit; as your fathers did, so do you. Which of the prophets did your fathers not persecute? And they killed those who foretold the coming of the Just One, of whom you now have become the betrayers and murderers, who have received the law by the direction of angels and have not kept it."** Steven told those people what they needed to hear, how that the prophecies of the Christ had been fulfilled in the one they knew to be Jesus of Nazareth whom they had caused to be crucified; the same message Peter delivered in Acts 2.

They didn't accept it so he said they were resisting the Holy Spirit. How in the world can man resist the Holy Spirit? He is divine. He is God. They did it the same way their fathers did. Their fathers persecuted and killed the prophets that had been sent to them for their own benefit, to show them the proper and true way of life. But specifically , they told of the coming of the Just One whom Steven says they had betrayed and killed. So, that is the way they resisted the Holy Spirit, by resisting or refusing to accept the message that the Holy Spirit , through the prophets, had delivered.

Look at the next statement which says they had received the law by or through angels and they resisted it and kept it not. You want to know how they resisted the Holy Spirit?; by not keeping the Law that He enabled the prophets to record for them. So, the Holy Spirit is named when in reality it is what the Holy Spirit directed the inspired men to speak and to write.

In Acts 2:33, Peter, in his sermon on the day of Pentecost said of Jesus: "Therefore being exalted to the right hand of God, and having received from the Father the promise of the Holy Spirit, He poured out this which you now see and hear." Jesus received the promise of the Holy Spirit. You know as well as I that it makes no sense to think that He received the Holy Spirit. There is a little tract that is published, I see it in a lot of racks from time to time, where the author cited Lenski on this passage where Lenski takes the position that Jesus received the Holy Spirit. Whether or not the author of that track intended to convey his belief that Jesus received the Holy Spirit is something you will have to decide but I can't help but wonder why he put it in there if he didn't believe it. That does not say that Jesus received the Holy Spirit. That says He received what the Holy Spirit had <u>promised</u>. What the Holy Spirit promised was that Christ would sit on David's throne. That passage is saying that at that very time Jesus was sitting on David's throne, reigning as "King of kings and Lord of lords". I remember when our brethren, when premillenniumism plagued the church, beat the socks off of them by citing this passage. On the day of Pentecost, nearly 2,000 years ago, Peter said Jesus was on the right hand of God where He received something. What He received was what the Holy Spirit promised; what the Holy Spirit promised was that He would sit on the throne of David. He was there! He received what the Holy Spirit promised in Psa. 132:11. So, the Holy Spirit may be referred to when His law or word is intended. These are facts. In logic, you establish a fact and then you are able to argue from that fact. Paul established the fact of the Resurrection in I Cor. 15 by pointing out that Jesus was raised from the dead. He did so by citing many witnesses. But some did not believe in the resurrection so he argued that if there was no resurrection then Jesus was not raised from the dead and our faith is in vain. Thus, by arguing from that which was proven, concerning the resurrection of Jesus, he concludes that there is indeed a resurrection of the dead.

Chart #11
SPECIAL MISSION OF THE HOLY SPIRIT (Jno 7:38-39)
IT MUST BE OBVIOUS TO ALL THAT THE SPIRIT HAD BEEN GIVEN BEFORE Jno. 7 & ACTS 2 Cf. "The Spirit of God came upon Saul..." I Sam. 11:6. "The Spirit of the Lord came upon David..." I Sam. 16:13 **THE BIBLE DOES NOT CONTRADICT ITSELF** HENCE: WE MUST UNDERSTAND THE LANGUAGE OF Jno. 7:39 TO MEAN THAT THE SPIRIT HAD NOT BEEN GIVEN IN THE SENSE & FOR THE PURPOSE OR MISSION CONTEMPLATED BY THE LORD
ABUSED BY CHARISMACTICS

Have you ever thought about the passages that you read concerning "all spiritual blessings are in Christ". In a very real sense we are living in the Spirit's age, in the Spirit's dispensation. You may reply "I thought it was the Age of Christ". It is but it is the Spirit's Law that directs us; the Spirit's Law; the gospel of Christ; the faith; the doctrine of Christ; the New Testament are all talking about the same message. But, the Holy Spirit had a special mission to accomplish. Look at this passage in Jno. 7:38-39: **"He who believes in Me, as the Scripture has said, out of his heart will flow rivers of living water."** But this He spoke concerning the Spirit, whom those believing in Him would receive; for the Holy Spirit was not yet given, because Jesus was not yet glorified. The KJV says "the Holy Ghost was not yet given", as I pointed out earlier to show that the "Holy Spirit" and "Holy Ghost" were terms used interchangeably. It should be obvious to all that the Holy Spirit had been given, there is no doubt about that: The Spirit of God came upon Saul, I Sam. 11:6; The Spirit of God came upon David, ISam.16:13. The bible does not contradict itself otherwise we could put no faith in what we read. Thus, I submit to you that we must understand the passage in Jno. 7 to mean that the Holy Spirit had not come to accomplish the special mission contemplated by the Lord. How else are you going to reconcile that statement without realizing that Jesus is pointing out that the Holy Spirit had a mission to accomplish and that He would come and fulfill that mission. This passage is abused by the Charismatics when they assume that it is talking about the Holy Spirit coming for the purpose of indwelling the body of each Christian.

Chart#12
MISSION OF THE HOLY SPIRIT CONTINUED
Jno. 16:7 "Nevertheless I tell you the truth: it is expedient for you that I go away; for if I go not away, the comforter will not come unto you; but if I go, I will send Him unto you" **NOTE:** Expedient that I GO AWAY! Why? If I go NOT AWAY the comforter WILL NOT COME! The coming of the Comforter, the Holy Spirit, was OBVIOUSLY IMPORTANT.
The Age of the Spirits Law (Rom. 8:2)

Here are those three passages that I mentioned to you earlier in Jno. 16. Let's look at them together. Jesus said in Jno. 14:26 (KJV) that the "Comforter" was the Holy Ghost so I know those two terms are the same, they are used interchangeably, the Comforter is the Holy Ghost. But we have already shown that the Holy Ghost is also the Holy Spirit. Therefore, the Comforter is the Holy Ghost which is the Holy Spirit.**"But**

the Comforter, which is the Holy Ghost, whom the Father will send in my name, he shall teach you all things, and bring all things to your remembrance, whatsoever I have said unto you." Now look in Jno.,15:26: **"But when the Comforter is come, whom I will send unto you from the Father, even the Spirit of truth, which proceedeth from the Father, he shall testify of me:"** We know that the Comforter is also the "Spirit of Truth". So, the Comforter is the "Spirit of Truth" , He is the Holy Ghost, and therefore the Holy Spirit. The Comforter is the revealer of truth and is named when what the Holy Spirit would do is intended. Jesus said that He will "testify and bear witness of Me".

Now turn to Jno. 16:13 where Jesus said to His Apostles: **"Howbeit when he, the Spirit of truth, is come, he will guide you into all truth: for he shall not speak of himself; but whatsoever he shall hear, that shall he speak: and he will shew you things to come."** So, the mission of the Holy Spirit was: 1) To teach all things; 2) To bring to their remembrance all that He had said; 3) To guide them into all truth; 4) To reveal things to come; and to bear witness. That was the purpose of signs and wonders. That was why they were called signs. A sign validates the man and the message, the revelation and confirmation of truth, which was the message of the Holy Spirit. If I ignore the mission of the Holy Spirit and reach some conclusion that is different from that mission, then I am making a mistake. I have and I am sure some of you have also pointed out that we need to understand the mission of Christ; why did He come? If it was for the purpose of making some social or political reform, then that is what we ought to be doing. But we pointed out that He came for the purpose of seeking and saving the lost. It was a spiritual mission. The church needs to recognize that its mission is a spiritual one, not a social or political or secular mission. The same thing is truth about the Holy Spirit's mission. We need to recognized that when we talk about what the Holy Spirit is doing, it had better agree with the reason He came, with His mission.

BASIC TRUTHS ABOUT THE HOLY SPIRIT

Now I want to summarize what we have learned and then the lesson will be yours. This chart illustrates what I have talked about this morning. I believe this is so basic to the understanding of the truth and I believe the reason some men have problems with it is because they don't start with the right concept .

Chart #13
BASIC TRUTHS
HOLY SPIRIT & HOLY GHOST ---SAME HOLY SPIRIT --- A PERSON * NOT "VAPOR" * NOT "IT" HOLY SPIRIT – DIVINE (ACTS 5:15) * HUMAN * ATTITUDE * HOLY SPIRIT 1. Cause for effect 2. Author for his writings (Spirit for His Law) 3. Miraculous effect Holy Spirit has a special mission: Revealing, Confirming & Recording the will of Christ.
ABOUT THE HOLY SPIRIT

1. I need to recognize that the Holy Spirit and the Holy Ghost are one and the same, not two different beings; not an it, not a vapor but a person just as the Father and Son are persons. The Holy Spirit is a divine person.
2. The term "Spirit" sometimes has reference to the human spirit, sometimes has reference to an attitude and sometimes has reference to the Holy Spirit.
3. We also need to realize that sometimes when the Holy Spirit is named, He is named for the cause when some effect is produced, as in the author for his writing and the Spirit for His Law.
4. Sometimes the word Holy Spirit has reference to some miraculous effect.
5. The Holy Spirit had a mission and that mission was to reveal and record the word of Christ. Just stop and think, in Jno. 16 Jesus said it is expedient for you that I go away. Think about that. He was with the

apostles but said to them that it was better that He go away and leave them. Why would it be better for Him to leave? He said it was a matter of expediency and explains why. He says "for if I go not away the Comforter will not come, but if I go away I will send Him". What is the Comforter, who is the Holy Spirit, going to do when He comes? He is going to reveal, confirm, and cause to be recorded the Will of Christ that teaches men how to be saved and how to live so that they might spend eternity with Him in heaven. That is why Christ said it was expedient for Him to go away.

6. The Holy Spirit had a mission to accomplish and He accomplished it; I have its accomplishment here today in this book. It tells me exactly what man must do in order to be right in the eyes of the Lord. The Spirit's Law says that a man has to come in faith believing that Jesus was the Son of God. If you don't believe that He was, then you will die in your sins. It tells me that I must repent of my sins, confess and be baptized and arise to walk in newness of life. It tells me that I am to put to death the deeds of the body that I might live; I am not to allow sin to reign in my mortal body and cause me to fulfill the lust there of. I must be faithful until death if I am to receive the crown of life. That is what the Spirit's Law reveals.

The End of Lesson One

CHAPTER TWO

"Holy Spirit Baptism"

Chart #14
BASIC TRUTHS
HOLY SPIRIT & HOLY GHOST ---SAME HOLY SPIRIT --- A PERSON * NOT "VAPOR" * NOT "IT" HOLY SPIRIT – DIVINE (Acts 5:15) * HUMAN * ATTITUDE * HOLY SPIRIT 1. Cause for effect 2. Author for his writings (Spirit for His Law) 3. Miraculous effect Holy Spirit has a special mission: Revealing, Confirming & Recording the will of Christ.
ABOUT THE HOLY SPIRIT

The Holy Spirit is a person, not a vapor, not it, but a person. Acts 5:1-5 states he is divine; thus he is a divine being. I suggested to you that when you take some position about the Holy Spirit, don't loose sight of the fact that you are talking about a divine being.

We've noted that the Bible uses the term "spirit" in the sense of the soul of man, a human spirit. It uses the term spirit to refer to an attitude or disposition, many times in the Bible this is the case. And, sometimes it's used to refer to the Holy Spirit. Sometimes when it's used as the Holy Spirit it's being used as the cause of some effect that's produced. For instance, the word of the Spirit produces certain things. Also, the author for his writings where the author is named and his writings are intended. The Spirits Law, the Spirit is named for his Law. And, sometimes it's named for some miraculous effect of the Holy Spirit. The Holy Spirit has a special mission and that mission is outlined for the revealing, the confirming and the recording of the will of Christ. Therefore, I need to remember and consider these matters when I study the subject of the Holy Spirit.

The subject at hand is Holy Spirit Baptism. This certainly is a Bible subject and there is no question about that. I will mention passages in the New Testament where it's referred to and I will only read one of them. It's referred to in: Mat. 3:11; Mk. 1:8; Lk. 3:16; Jno. 1:33; Acts 1: 5; Acts 11:16.

Let's read the account in Mat. 3 and we'll use that as a background for our study about this Bible subject. This is the occasion when Jesus came to be baptized of John in the river Jordan, and this is in Mark and Luke as well, The record tells us in verse 11:

I indeed baptize you in water unto repentance: but he that cometh after me is mightier than I, whose shoes I am not worthy to bear: he shall baptize you in the Holy Spirit and {in} fire: 12 whose fan is in his hand, and he will thoroughly cleanse his threshing-floor; and he will gather his wheat into the garner, but the chaff he will burn up with unquenchable fire.

Chart #15
MATTHEW 3:9-12
" ... For I say to you that God is able to raise up children to Abraham from these stones. And even now the ax is laid to the root of the trees. Therefore every tree which does not bear good fruit is cut down and thrown into the **fire**. **I** indeed baptize you with water unto repentance, but **He** who is coming after me is mightier than **I**, whose sandals I am not worthy to carry. **He** will baptize you with the Holy Spirit and **fire**. "His winnowing fan is in **His** hand, and **He** will thoroughly purge **His** threshing floor, and gather His wheat into the barn; but **He** will burn up the chaff with unquenchable **fire**."
ADMINISTRATOR: NOT SUBJECTS!

We are talking about a Bible subject here, no doubt about it. We have already learned, in the previous lesson, that the Holy Spirit came through the Lord's promise; guided the apostles into all truth and reminded them of the things that Christ had taught them. He declared the things to come and also promised to validate, verify that message, Jno. 14:26, Jno. 15:26 and Jno. 16 :12 -14. I want to read with you in Jno. 16:12-14: **"I have yet many things to say unto you, but ye cannot bear them now. 13 Howbeit when he, the Spirit of truth, is come, he shall guide you into all the truth: for he shall not speak from himself; but what things soever he shall hear, {these} shall he speak: and he shall declare unto you the things that are to come. 14 He shall glorify me: for he shall take of mine, and shall declare {it} unto you."** In this text we see that the Holy Spirit is responsible for this book, the Bible. Whatever the Holy Spirit says about Holy Spirit baptism, that's the truth! This is what I must accept about it. I cannot rely on men. You try to do that and you can't imagine how many difficulties you will have. This is why I have difficulty understanding how the religious world in general will rely on what men tell them about this and not recognize that these men are woefully divided as to the purpose or design of Holy Spirit baptism. Even those who claim to be spirit filled and guided are woefully divided. For instance, the Assemblies of God, a group that claims to be able to perform signs and wonders, believe that they have Holy Spirit baptism. Their concept of Holy Spirit baptism is that it is a second work of grace, it comes after salvation, that one is saved by "faith only". Then, later on, they receive Holy Spirit baptism. This is their concept. The United Pentecostal's concept is that the spirit of the new birth is Holy Spirit baptism and that the water of the new birth is water baptism. Therefore, one is not saved, is not born again, unless he is baptized in the Holy Spirit and had water baptism.

Now, let's look at these two views. One of them says that Holy Spirit baptism is necessary to salvation and the other one says that Holy Spirit baptism is the result of salvation. These two groups don't seem to be embarrassed about the fact that they are woefully divided on this. I have certainly longed for an opportunity to attend a debate between them where they try to work this thing out. I don't believe it's ever going to happen. You don't determine the truth from purely subjectivism. By that I mean the way that you feel about something. You know, feelings will lead you astray. We feel the way we do because of what we believe. We believe what we do because of certain evidence. If the evidence we have is not reliable then our feelings will misguide us. This is true of our subject. People have a "feeling" about this, they just know they say, it's a subjective thing with them. We need to understand who was promised and who received Holy Spirit baptism. We need to understand why they received it and the purpose for it. We'll try to find out and also how long it was to continue. I submit to you that just by finding the word "spirit" does not mean you have found a passage dealing with Holy Spirit baptism. Whenever you look at a passage, it must be labeled Holy Spirit baptism either by name or by description. If it is not then you don't have the right to make it mean Holy Spirit baptism. That is what these fellows will do. They find a passage that talks about the spirit; they automatically decide that it is the Holy Spirit, which is the first mistake they make. The second mistake is that after they have assumed the word "spirit" means Holy Spirit, they then assume it means Holy Spirit baptism. You don't assume that, you have to prove it. These are the things we need to understand. Mind control is certainly a fact that we understand and we know that it happens. So many times this is what takes place. Men will absolutely try to control our mind and make a passage say something it does not say.

When the Jews came out to John to be baptized, at the end he said to them, (Mat 3:9): **"and think not to say within yourselves, We have Abraham to our father: for I say unto you, that God is able of these stones to raise up children unto Abraham."** Incidentally, there are those who seem to think that God is doing everything that he is able to do but he's not is he. That is fallacious reasoning. The idea is that God is doing everything he is able to do. No, he is not, he can limit his power and thank God for that because that passage says he is able, he has the ability to raise up seed unto Abraham from stones. He said: **"And now also the axe is laid unto the root of the trees: therefore every tree which bringeth not forth good fruit is hewn down, and cast into the fire. 11 I indeed baptize you with water unto repentance: but he that cometh after me is mightier than I, whose shoes I am not worthy to bear: he shall baptize you with the Holy Ghost, and with fire: 12 Whose fan is in his hand, and he will throughly purge his floor, and gather his wheat into the garner; but he will burn up the chaff with unquenchable fire.**" (Mat. 3:10 –12)

They take this and make it mean a universal promise. That passage doesn't tell you who will receive Holy Spirit baptism. If it has to do with those present earlier in that chapter, he has said, you generation of vipers, who has warned you to flee from the wrath to come? Were they the ones who were promised Holy Spirit baptism? This passage is not talking about who will receive Holy Spirit baptism; it is talking about <u>who will administer it</u>! We have allowed them to simply take our mind and make us see what they want that passage to say. That doesn't tell you who is going to be baptized! It tells who is going to do it! John said he could baptize them with water but there is someone who can do more than that. He that comes after me is mightier than I. I'm not even worthy to bear his shoes. It is he who will baptize you with the Holy Ghost and with fire. While I'm on this text, a person, a writer or anyone else, that uses a term consistently in any discourse and doesn't use it with the same meaning is making a serious mistake. You don't do that. The word "fire" obviously is being used in the same sense throughout this text. In verse 10, he talks about "hewn down and cast into fire", then he says "baptized in the Holy Spirit and with fire". Look at the next passage, **"and will burn up the chaff with unquenchable fire"**. That is talking about "unquenchable fire". I don't have any doubt about it. It's talking about the fact of eternal hell. I see men go out and make some kind of explanation about this, about literal Israel. You don't have the right to do that in a text, making it figurative when you don't have to because there is such a thing as unquenchable fire. I know what that's talking about. A speaker or writer is not going to use a term in one sense in any discourse and then the same term in another sense without telling you that he is changing its application. In this instance he's obviously using fire in the same way. You have three verses, verse 10, 11, and 12 where the same word occurs in all three and Jesus tells you what kind of fire He is talking about and it's not one kind of fire in verse 10 and another kind of fire in verse 12. An honest speaker or writer does not violate that basic rule. Therefore, in the text he indicates two things that the Lord is powerful enough to do; to baptize man in the Holy Spirit and also baptize him in fire. This is talking about the administrator, it's not talking about the subject and don't let someone twist your mind and tell you that this passage says <u>who</u> is going to be baptized. In Jno. 1:33, John declares:

"And I knew him not: but he that sent me to baptize with water, the same said unto me, Upon whom thou shalt see the Spirit descending, and remaining on him, the same is he which baptizeth with the Holy Ghost." I know whom the administrator of Holy Spirit baptism is. It's Jesus. There is not any question about it. Man cannot do that, Jesus is the administrator of Holy Spirit baptism. Keep this in mind as we continue to look at these passages.

FILLED WITH THE SPIRIT

There are those who tell us that to be filled with the Spirit means to be baptized in the Holy Spirit and they cite Acts 2 :1 -4. We'll go through these passages as we talk about them. The record says:

"And when the day of Pentecost was now come, they were all together in one place.And suddenly there came from heaven a sound as of the rushing of a mighty wind, and it filled all the house where they were sitting. And there appeared unto them tongues parting asunder, like as of fire; and it sat upon each one of them. And they were all filled with the Holy Spirit, and began to speak with other tongues, as the Spirit gave them utterance."

The passage says they were filled with the Holy Spirit. The Pentecostals say: "Now you folks recognize Holy Spirit baptism and Holy Spirit baptism and filled with the Holy Spirit are used interchangeably. To be filled with the Spirit, that's Holy Spirit baptism. " We will study this long and hard to make sure we get all the facts in the case.

There's not any question, in this instance, that being filled with the Holy Spirit was Holy Spirit baptism; but does that mean everywhere the Bible talks about being filled with the Spirit, that it is Holy Spirit baptism? Let's see if that's the case. Turn to Lk. 1:15. These folks tell us that Holy Spirit baptism is the spirit of the new birth and the initial act is speaking in tongues. Speaking in tongues is the thing that follows Holy Spirit baptism according to them. In Lk. 1:15, it's talking about John the Baptist:

"For he shall be great in the sight of the Lord and he shall drink no wine or strong drink and he shall be filled with the Holy Spirit, even from his mother's womb".

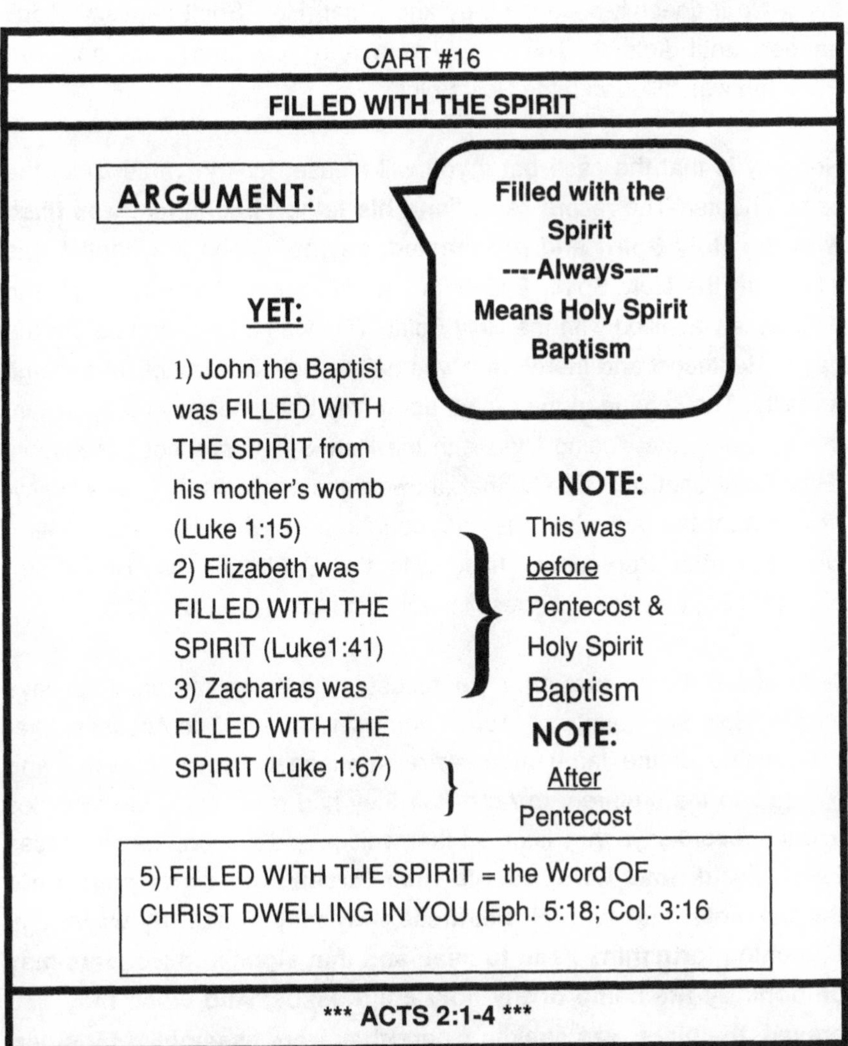

Now then, was John the Baptist baptized in the Holy Spirit even before Holy Spirit baptism was promised? These folks know better than that! They will admit that, in fact I have used that in dispute with them. Look if you will in Lk. 1:41. The record says of Elizabeth: **"and it came to pass when Elizabeth had heard the salutation of Mary, the babe leaped in her womb and Elizabeth was filled with the Holy Spirit"** Therefore, Elizabeth was filled with the Holy Spirit. Was she baptized in the Holy Spirit? They tell us that since Acts 2:1-4 indicates that when the apostles were baptized in the Holy Spirit, they were filled with it; therefore, "to be filled with the spirit" and "Holy Spirit baptism" always means the same thing. No it doesn't, because they know that "Holy Spirit baptism" didn't happen until Acts 2. They know that and you know that and yet, Elizabeth was "filled with the Holy Spirit".

Not only is that the case but if you will please, look in verse 67 of the same chapter. The record says: **"and his father, Zacharias, was filled with the Holy Spirit and prophesied, saying"**. John the Baptist was filled with the Holy Spirit, Elizabeth was filled with the Holy Spirit and Zacharias was filled with the Holy Spirit. This was a long time before the day of Pentecost and therefore it was before Holy Spirit baptism became a reality. They changed their mind about this because they recognize in, this instance, that "being filled with the Holy Spirit" was not necessarily "Holy Spirit baptism". Really, that answers their argument. They will say, (this is after the fact when they get caught in it), what they really meant was that after Pentecost, "filled with the Spirit" means "Holy Spirit baptism". So, they know it doesn't mean it in Lk. 1:15, 41 and 67.

Let's see if it's so that after Pentecost, "filled with the spirit" always means "Holy Spirit baptism". Turn if you will to Acts 4. The Apostles, after the healing of the lame man, were imprisoned, were released and returned to the brethren. In Acts 4:31 they had returned to the disciples and the record says they lifted up their voices and prayed, then in verses 29-31: **"And now, Lord, behold their threatenings: and grant unto thy servants, that with all boldness they may speak thy word, By stretching forth thine hand to heal; and that signs and wonders may be done by the name of thy holy child Jesus. And when they had prayed, the place was shaken where they were assembled together; and they were all filled with the Holy Ghost, and they spake the word of God with boldness."** Now then, the question is this. These apostles who were filled with the Holy Spirit on the day of Pentecost, do you think they were baptized by the Holy Spirit again? Do you see what I am saying? These apostles were baptized in the Holy Spirit and were said to be "filled with the Holy Spirit" in Acts 2 and now we read in Acts 4:31 that they were "filled with the Holy Spirit" again! The question is: "Did they have to have a re-filling?" No! They have a total misconception of what "filled with the Spirit" means.

John the Baptist, Elizabeth, and Zecharias were filled with the spirit but that doesn't mean Holy Spirit baptism. This is a cause and effect situation. This was not Holy Spirit baptism in Acts 4:31. The record says the place was shaken wherein they were and not only that, they prayed **"Lord grant unto thy servants that we may speak the word with boldness".** There was evidence then that their cry was heard, that's what the record indicates. The Holy Spirit is named for a gift or the operation of the Spirit. What happened is, the place where they were at was shaken and as a consequence they spoke the word boldly, the very thing that they prayed that they might be able to do. Note if you will what I have tried to point out. There are those who say filled with the Spirit always means Holy Spirit baptism. Yet, whenever you point to the fact that they don't accept what they argue "well after the day of Pentecost it always meant Holy Spirit baptism". Incidentally, in these passages where you read about John the Baptist Elizabeth and Zacharias, you will note that immediately after this, especially with Elizabeth and Zacharias, they were filled with the Holy Spirit and they prophesied. Again you have a cause and effect situation where the Holy Spirit is named for what the Holy Spirit enabled them to do. It's a total mistake to assume that it means Holy Spirit baptism.

Let's look at Eph. 5:18. These are passages that you are acquainted with where the writer, Paul, talks about singing. He said: **"Be not drunken with wine wherein is strife but be filled with the spirit, speaking one to another in songs and hymns and spiritual songs, singing and making melody with your heart to the Lord".** Now, look if you will, at Col. 3:16. These are companion passages. Many times when you are reading the book of Ephesians and you run across a passage that you have difficulty understanding, look at the Colossian letter, you will probably find the same subject being discussed and it will clarify the statement to some degree. Therefore, the same writer is discussing this same subject as he writes to the Colossians in Col. 3 :16.

Now, in Eph. 5:18 he says be filled with the Spirit. Look what he says in Col. 3:16. **"Let the word of Christ dwell in you richly"**. Is he teaching two different things? No, he just tells you how man is filled with the Spirit; **"filled with the spirit"** (Eph. 5), and **"let the word of Christ dwell in**

you", (Col. 3:16). Therefore, filled with the Spirit does not always mean Holy Spirit baptism.

Chart #17
Ephesians 5:18-21 And do not be drunk with wine, in which is dissipation; but be filled with the Spirit, speaking to one another in psalms and hymns and spiritual songs, singing and making melody in your heart to the Lord, giving thanks always for all things to God the Father in the name of our Lord Jesus Christ, submitting to one another in the fear of God.
Colossians 3:16-17 Let the word of Christ dwell in you richly in all wisdom, teaching and admonishing one another in psalms and hymns and spiritual songs, singing with grace in your hearts to the Lord. And whatever you do in word or deed, do all in the name of the Lord Jesus, giving thanks to God the Father through Him.

I would like to make this observation, now, as we continue in these studies. When the Spirit's Law, the word of God, the gospel of Christ, is in a man's heart, directing his thinking and directing his life, he is being filled with the Spirit, he's being led by the Spirit; the Spirit of God is dwelling in him through that medium, the Spirit's Law. So, even though Holy Spirit baptism is said to be filled with the Spirit, it doesn't always mean that "filled with the Spirit" is "Holy Spirit baptism". The point I'm making is when you find a passage in one instance where Holy Spirit baptism is said to be something and find that same something somewhere else and assume that's Holy Spirit baptism also, it becomes a matter of confusion. I think the illustration of the animal kingdom I mentioned makes my point. You see a horse and call it an animal and then argue an animal is a horse; it does not follow.

Now then, who would receive Holy Spirit baptism? Why would they receive it and for how long? Will you turn with me to Mat.10 and we will examine some passages. I suggested to you that it either had to be named or labeled such. Let's look at verse 1: **"And when he had called unto him his twelve disciples, he gave them power against unclean spirits, to cast them out, and to heal all manner of sickness and all manner of disease."** The apostles are named, he sends them forth and then in verse 16 we read: **"Behold, I send you forth as sheep in the midst of wolves: be ye therefore wise as serpents, and harmless as doves. 17 But beware of men: for they will deliver you up to the councils, and they will scourge you in their synagogues; 18 And ye shall be brought before governors and kings for my sake, for a testimony against them and the Gentiles. 19 But when they deliver you up, take no thought how or what ye shall speak: for it shall be given you in that same hour what ye shall speak. 20 For it is not ye that speak, but the Spirit of your Father which speaketh in you."** May I suggest to you that those who claim Holy Spirit baptism do not deny that this is talking about Holy Spirit baptism. Every one of them will agree that is talking about Holy Spirit baptism and I believe it is talking about the time after they are baptized by the Holy Spirit. Who was Holy Spirit baptism promised to? This is the thing I want you to see. In Mat. 10:1 he called his twelve disciples. He said now in the latter part of chapter 10: 40: **"He that receiveth you receiveth me, and he that receiveth me receiveth him that sent me. He that receiveth a prophet in the name of a prophet shall receive a prophet's reward; and he that receiveth a righteous man in the name of a righteous man shall receive a righteous man's reward."** That simply indicates you receive a prophet because of what he is and a righteous man because of what he is. The word "name" is used in the Bible to refer to reputation and character. Obviously, here it is used in the sense of character. You receive him because of what he is, not what he looks like.

Let's continue on in chapter 11 verse 1: **"And it came to pass, when Jesus had made an end of commanding his twelve disciples, he departed thence to teach and to preach in their cities."** It doesn't take Solomon to see who he is talking to does it? Mat. 10 verse 1 says Jesus called unto him his twelve disciples. He had a long discussion with them, sent them out, then chapter 11 says it came to pass when Jesus had finished commanding his twelve disciples he departed to teach and preach in cities. Therefore, to whom did he make the promise in verse

16? He made it to the apostles. The promise was made to his ambassadors, the apostles, and people want to claim that promise for themselves. In this instance it is obvious Jesus was with the twelve apostles.

Chart #18
THE PROMISE OF THE HOLY SPIRIT
Acts 1:1-8
Act 1:1-5 The former treatise I made, O Theophilus, concerning all that Jesus began both to do and to teach,until the day in which he was received up, after that he had given commandment through the Holy Spirit unto the apostles whom he had chosen: To whom he also showed himself alive after his passion by many proofs, appearing unto them by the space of forty days, and speaking the things concerning the kingdom of God: and, being assembled together with them, he charged them not to depart from Jerusalem, but to wait for the promise of the Father, which, {said he,} ye heard from me: For John indeed baptized with water; but ye shall be baptized in the Holy Spirit not many days hence.
THE ASCENTION
6-8 They therefore, when they were come together, asked him, saying, Lord, dost thou at this time restore the kingdom to Israel? And he said unto them, It is not for you to know times or seasons, which the Father hath set within His own authority. But ye shall receive power, when the Holy Spirit is come upon you: and ye shall be my witnesses both in Jerusalem, and in all Judaea and Samaria, and unto the uttermost part of the earth.

Another passage where Holy Spirit baptism is mentioned is in Acts 1: 1-3; the writer of the book of Acts identifies the fact that he had written something prior to this. He is obviously talking about the book of Luke. Look at the text. There are two or three things I want to emphasize here with you. First of all the record says that he had given commandment to the apostles whom he had chosen. What the writer, Luke, does is to go back and pick up the statement he made in Lk. 24:46-49 where Jesus said: **"And said unto them, Thus it is written, and thus it behoved Christ to suffer, and to rise from the dead the third day: 47 And that**

repentance and remission of sins should be preached in his name among all nations, beginning at Jerusalem. :48 And ye are witnesses of these things. 49 And, behold, I send the promise of my Father upon you: but tarry ye in the city of Jerusalem, until ye be endued with power from on high." This is what he is talking about here and do you know whom he was with when that statement was made? He was with eleven of His apostles, Mk. 16:14. That is when he appeared unto the eleven as they themselves testified. The point is that the language of Lk. 24:46-49 is comparable to Mat. 28:18-20 and Mk. 16:15-16. We know full well that it is talking about the same thing, the Great Commission, and that it was given to the apostles!

Now, look at this, if you will. He's talking about the apostles whom he had chosen. What does the "to whom" of (1:3) have reference to? The apostles, that's what it has reference to. **"To be seen of them",** "them" is a pronoun and grammatically a pronoun refers back to the previous noun unless it's impossible for it to do so. Those folks ignore this and pay no attention to the grammar of the text. He is talking about the same ones; he commanded them not to depart from Jerusalem. In Lk. 24 he said to tarry in the city until they were endowed with power from on high. Here Jesus said they were not to depart from Jerusalem. Now watch what He said: **"for John truly baptized with water but ye shall be baptized with the Holy Ghost not many days hence"**. The text in Matthew is a general statement about what the Lord was capable of doing, baptize in the Holy Spirit and in fire. The recipients are not identified there. In this text they are identified and you'll read until you go stone blind trying to find fire in it. I think that is significant and I think people need to understand that. The record says when they, now who is that talking about? That's talking about the "them", it's talking about the "who", it's talking about the apostles! You would have to throw away the rules of grammar to think otherwise.

When these fellows claim this passage for themselves, I say to them, why don't you do what he says? Are you in Jerusalem? That's where they were to be. You see, they take that passage and claim it, and he said you tarry in Jerusalem because that's where it's going to take place. Not only is that the case, He said, then when that happens you are to be my witness in Jerusalem, Judea and Samaria. Are they doing that, are they witnessing in those places? No, but the apostles did! Therefore, I submit to you that you have the recipients of Holy Spirit baptism identified in this text. It was the “apostles” and no "fire” is mentioned at that point.

Chart # 19
Acts 1&2
Acts 1:26 And they cast their lots, and the lot fell on Matthias. And he was numbered with the eleven apostles. **THE HOLY SPIRIT COMES AT PENTECOST (Acts2:1-4)** And when the day of Pentecost was now come, they were all together in one place. And suddenly there came from heaven a sound as of the rushing of a mighty wind, and it filled all the house where they were sitting. And there appeared unto them tongues parting asunder, like as of fire; and it sat upon each one of them. And they were all filled with the Holy Spirit, and began to speak with other tongues, as the Spirit gave them utterance.

In Acts 1:26, after the ascension of the Lord, they went back into the city of Jerusalem and there they tarried. Incidentally for what it is worth to you, where there is a will there has to be a properly qualified executor of that will. Those men, the apostles, were qualified, that is what it says. You are to be my witness but you are to be endowed with power in order to do this. They were empowered to execute his will; to make it known.

In Acts 1, they went back into Jerusalem like he had told them to and there they tarried. It was necessary for someone to be selected to take the place of Judas and the record tells us that Matthias was selected and he was numbered with the eleven apostles. Chapters and verses were added by translators and I'm certainly thankful that they were. They were put there so we could identify this. Whenever the scriptures were written they didn't have chapters and verses like we have now. Therefore, if you just look at this the record says, **“and they drew forth their lot and the lot fell upon Matthias and he was numbered with the eleven apostles”**. Now watch this. **“And when the day of Pentecost fully**

come, they", now what does that have reference to? There are those who go all the way back in the text where it is said there were approximately 120 disciples that tarried there in the upper chamber. They say that's where that took place and therefore all120 were baptized by the Holy Spirit.

If you ever wrote them a letter you couldn't use pronouns, they wouldn't know what you were talking about. I have had debates with an audience of 1000 people, a lot of them teenagers, and you know those teenagers knew what I was talking about. They were in school and they knew full well that when you have a pronoun you need to determine the noun preceding it. You don't just go back to any noun you want. You go to the immediately preceding noun. Therefore, the record tells us that when the day of Pentecost had fully come "they", now to whom is he talking about? It was the "twelve apostles". The record says "they" were all together, with one accord and suddenly there came a sound from heaven as a rushing mighty wind and it filled all the house where "they" were sitting and there appeared unto "them" cloven tongues like as fire that set upon each one of "them" and "they" were all filled with the Holy Ghost and began to speak with other tongues as the Spirit gave "them" utterance. There is no way that a person can read that intelligently and fail to see that the apostles were the ones who were baptized in the Holy Spirit on the day of Pentecost. The record says in Acts 2:4 that those who were filled with the Holy Spirit began to speak. **"And they were all filled with the Holy Ghost, and began to speak with other tongues, as the Spirit gave them utterance".** Here's the form of a logical argument. <u>All</u> that were filled with the Holy Spirit spoke. Only the apostles <u>spoke</u>, (v14). Therefore, only the apostles were <u>filled</u> with the Holy Spirit. Look at verse 14. **"But Peter standing up with the 11, lifted up his voice".** All that was baptized in the Holy Spirit spoke! The apostles were those that spoke, therefore the apostles were the ones filled with the Holy Spirit on the day of Pentecost. The passage says that <u>all</u> that were filled with the Holy Spirit began to speak as the Spirit gave them utterance. Who did the speaking? It was the twelve apostles

CHART #20

POWER

"But you shall receive power when the Holy Spirit has come upon you; and you shall be witnesses to Me in Jerusalem, and in all Judea and Samaria, and to the end of the earth." **Acts 1:8**

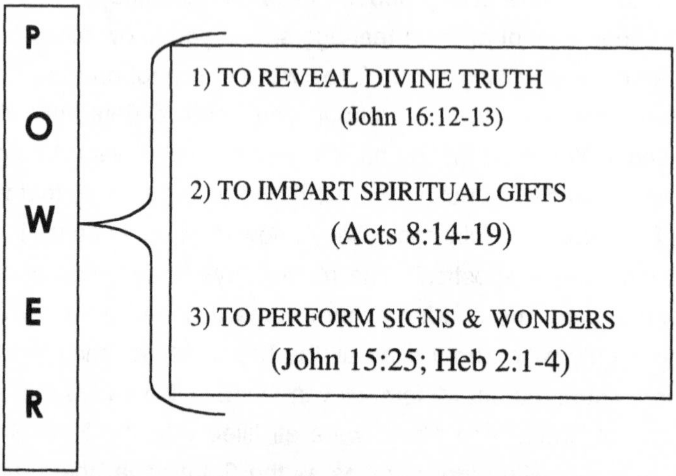

P O W E R

1) TO REVEAL DIVINE TRUTH
(John 16:12-13)

2) TO IMPART SPIRITUAL GIFTS
(Acts 8:14-19)

3) TO PERFORM SIGNS & WONDERS
(John 15:25; Heb 2:1-4)

ACTS 1:8

Not only is that the case but the apostles were the ones that performed signs and wonders. In Acts 2, the record tells us in verse 43 that many signs and wonders were done through the apostles. In Acts 3 you have the healing of the lame man and in that instance there was the miracle of healing, verses 1 through 10. Who did that? The apostles did. Look at Acts 5:12 : **"And by the hands of the apostles were many signs and wonders wrought among the people; ".** Some folks will say that doesn't prove anything. It does prove something! There's an implication in this. Signs and wonders were wrought by those who had the ability to do it. Who had that ability? All of the apostles had that ability. You don't read about anyone else that performed a sign or wonder until after the hands of the apostles had been laid upon the seven in Acts 6 and then the record says **"Steven wrought great signs and wonders among the people"**. Up to that point in time only the apostles performed signs and wonders. I think there is evidence of such in II Cor. 12:12, where the apostle Paul said to the Corinthians: **"Truly the signs of an apostle were wrought among you in all patience, in signs, and wonders, and mighty deeds.** " Who received Holy Spirit baptism? The apostles received Holy Spirit baptism. Why did they receive it? We don't have to guess about that. We are told in no uncertain terms. Jesus said to them in Acts 1 that they would receive power after the Holy Spirit came upon them. It was to be the power that enabled them to reveal divine truth, (Jno. 16:12-13). To reveal simply means to uncover. They were able to make known, uncover, and reveal divine truth. They could also impart miraculous gifts of the Spirit.

Philip, one of the seven that had the apostles hands laid upon him, went down to Samaria and preached to them and performed signs and wonders and the people gave heed to him when they heard and saw the signs which he did. He could not impart that gift to others. The record says when the church at Jerusalem heard that the Samaritans had received the word, they sent to them Peter and John. Note if you will, when the bible tells of someone being sent and doesn't tell you why, see what they did when they got there, then you know why they were sent. That is the principle of truth. What did the apostles do? They laid their hand upon them that they might receive the Holy Spirit. When Simon saw that by laying on of their hands the Holy Spirit was given he desired that power for himself. More about that when we talk about miraculous gifts. So, they were given the power to impart gifts of the Spirit and also to perform signs and wonders,(Heb. 2:1-4; Jno. 15:25). That has to do with the apostles.

CORNELIUS' CONVERSION

I believe that Cornelius received Holy Spirit baptism and I want to show you that he did and why he received it. Turn with me, if you will, to Acts the Eleventh Chapter. As in the case of the conversion of Saul (Paul), you have more than one account given in the scriptures. That is why it is important to go to all accounts in order to get the whole truth. In the 10th chapter you have an historical account of the conversion. In the 11th chapter you have an explanation of Peter's reason for going to those gentiles in the first place. I want you to note now in, Acts 11, the reason I say to you that this was Holy Spirit baptism .

Chart #21
CORNELIUS' CONVERSION: **-- IN ORDER --**
DEFINITION: "With the significance of a succession of events, an event following in order after another" (W.E. Vine, pg. 43, #2&3) **NOTE SUCCESSION OF EVENTS:** - - Peter explains his action - - 1) The Vision Acts 11:5-10 2) Three men from Cornelias - V11 3) The Holy Spirit told him to go - V12 4) He took six brethren with him - V13 5) An angel told Cornelius to send for Peter V13 6) As he "began to speak": the Holy Spirit fell on Cornelius like at the beginning V 5, Acts 2
WENT - - - PREACHED - - - BAPTIZED- - - ATE **(Acts10-11:18)**

Begin with me in verse 12 and read down through verse 15. Peter said: " **And the Spirit bade me go with them, making no distinction. And these six brethren also accompanied me; and we entered into the man's house: and he told us how he had seen the angel standing in his house, and saying, Send to Joppa, and fetch Simon, whose surname is Peter; who shall speak unto thee words, whereby thou shalt be saved, thou and all thy house. And as I began to speak, the Holy Spirit fell on them, even as on us at the beginning.**" The beginning of what? The beginning of this age, this dispensation. Keep this in mind. He had to go all the way back to the day of Pentecost of Acts 2 to find another case like this. If people had been baptized in the Holy Spirit every time they were converted, why did Peter say, **"the Holy Spirit fell on them as upon on us at the beginning**" ? Get the force of that statement. He couldn't find another case like it since the time the apostles were baptized by the Holy Spirit in the beginning, on the day of Pentecost. Not only does that indicate he had to go all the way back to

Acts 2, but watch what he says: "**And as I began to speak, the Holy Spirit fell upon them, as upon us at the beginning.** Then Peter remembered something; "**Then I remembered the word of the Lord, how He said, 'John indeed baptized with water, but you shall be baptized with the Holy Spirit.'** Peter said it reminded him of Holy Spirit baptism. Why would I deny that? Let me tell you what has been said. I have been told that, "Well if you admit that, you weaken your position with the Charismatic". Is that the criteria that we use to determine what the truth is? I resent that. I have heard men make that statement that had never met a Charismatic in debate. It is a personal offense to me to say that I weaken my defense against them when I debate them and took this position on Cornelius. I take the position on Cornelius because that is what the passage says. The Holy Spirit "fell on them even as on us in the beginning" and then Peter said I remembered the promise of Holy Spirit baptism. Someone said, "Well if he was baptized by the Holy Spirit he could do all that the apostles did." Who said so? See, they just pluck this out of the air. There were nine different spiritual gifts, (I Cor.12). All of these came by the same source, the laying on of the apostle's hands. But they didn't all do the same thing did they? Some spoke in tongues, some were able to interpret, some had miraculous faith, some could prophecy &etc. My point is this, the argument brethren have made will not hold water. They say that if Cornelius received Holy Spirit baptism then he would be able to do all that the apostles did. No, because there were those that had the apostles hands laid on them and received a gift from the Holy Spirit and they could not do all that the others could do, (I Cor. 12:4-11; 12:29). The Holy Spirit provided something for Cornelius and the bible tells us exactly why the Holy Spirit fell on him. It was for the purpose of convincing the Jews that God had indeed accepted the Gentiles. Peter had to make use of this very argument when he returned to Jerusalem and faced his Jewish brethren.

ACTS 10 VERSUS ACTS 11

(The Order Of Occurrence versus Order Of Record)

With that in mind we need to recognize that the order of record is not always the order of occurrence. What am I saying? When you read of certain events in the bible that are given in a certain order, that does not necessarily mean that the events happened in exactly that precise order.

You assume that the order is the same as the occurrence in a given passage but if another passage gives you another account of the event in question and this account is said to be in order of occurrence and it is not the same order as the first account then, you know the first account was not the order of occurrence. Let me show you what I mean. Look in Acts 11:4: **"But Peter explained it to them in order from the beginning"** Brethren who make arguments like they do on Holy Spirit baptism need to meet those who deny the essentiality of water baptism. One of the arguments they make is on Cornelius and the only way you can repudiate their argument is to recognize the order of events in the conversion. Now what did it mean to "explain the events in order". It was important . Acts 10 does not relate the same events in the same order as in Acts 11.

Peter met with the house of Cornelius, ate with them and baptized them into Christ . When he returned to Jerusalem those that were of the circumcision contended with him. They asked why did you go? Peter wanted to make it very clear to them why he went. Do you remember the vision that he had on the house top? The Holy Spirit bade him go with the men doubting nothing. He took six brethren with him for a witness. When they asked why he went he said I am going to tell you why I went. So, he relates the events in succession. Following in order after another, that's what that word "order" means.

Notice the order of events: 1. There was the vision, (Acts 11:5-10); 2. There were three men who had come from Cornelius, (V 11); 3. The Holy Spirit told him to go, (V 13); 4. He took six brethren with him, (V 13); 5. An angel told Cornelius to send for Peter, (V 13); 6. As he "began to speak", the Holy Spirit fell upon Cornelius like at the beginning, (V 15). The Holy Spirit fell upon Cornelius before Peter preached to him. If the events as given in Acts 10 was all there was you might think that the Holy Spirit fell upon him sometime during the sermon. But this said **"as I began to speak"** and that means, literally, scarcely had I uttered a word when this happened. So, he went, he preached, he baptized and then he ate.

Why did I say that the given order of events and the order of occurrence is not necessarily the same? Because in Acts 10 the order of events are not in the same order as Peter explains them in Chapter 11. I would have a problem with that if it were not for the fact that this passage says the writer did give the events in the order that they occurred. There was a reason for it. In Acts 10, Luke was merely giving an historical account, the order was not important. This is why I suggested to you, brethren, that a study of bible hermeneutics, the science of interpretation, is important. It is a fact that the order of record is not necessarily the order of occurrence. Here is an instance where that is obviously so. If you have read my recent debate published in the Guardian of Truth on the "cup" question this idea was discussed at length. Let me show you another case in point so that you will know that I am not just plucking this out of the air. In Rom. 10:9, Paul said: **"that if you confess with your mouth the Lord Jesus and believe in your heart that God has raised Him from the dead, you will be saved."** Is that the proper order of confession and belief? Do you confess before you believe? No, the order of record is not always the order of occurrence. The language demands this and I am saying to you that the language of Acts 11 also demands that the order of record is precisely as Peter indicated. He had a reason for doing that. Why did the Holy Spirit fall upon Cornelius? Well, it wasn't to save him because the record says that he was to "**hear words whereby you might be saved**" and the Holy Spirit fell on him before he heard those words. So, it didn't fall on him to save him and it didn't fall on him to produce faith. Incidentally, there is an account in Acts 15:7-9 also, of this incident. When the Apostle Peter declared: **"And when there had been much questioning, Peter rose up, and said unto them, Brethren, ye know that a good while ago God made choice among you, that by my mouth the Gentiles should hear the word of the gospel, and believe. And God, who knoweth the heart, bare them witness, giving them the Holy Spirit, even as he did unto us; and he made no distinction between us and them, cleansing their hearts by faith.** So, it was not to produce faith because Peter said the Gentiles should hear the word of the gospel and believe it. My point is they had to hear the gospel in order to believe and that faith produced by what they heard purified theirs hearts. The purpose was to convince the Jews that God would accept the Gentiles, and to give assurance to the Gentiles.

Stop and think with me for a minute. All this took place before the Gentiles heard the gospel. You would think that the church would be willing to preach it to just anybody but that was not so because of the prejudice that existed between the Jews and Gentiles. They had to be convinced and it took these miracles to do it. First of all it took the miracles on the house top; It took the fact that the Holy Spirit told Peter "you go doubting nothing". The Apostle Peter recognized the possibility of problems so he took six brethren with him. When he arrived at the house of Cornelius, he was told how an angel had appeared unto him and told him to send for Peter. Peter went through those events with the church at Jerusalem.

Notice then, in Acts 11:18, **"when they heard this"** , that is, when he had finished relating these matters in order, talking about all the miracles that caused him to go and what happened when he arrived and how the Holy Spirit fell on them even as on us in the beginning. Then Peter said in verse 17: **"If therefore God gave them the same gift as He gave us when we believed on the Lord Jesus Christ, who was I that I could withstand God?"** In other words it convinced the Jews that God would accept the Gentiles. That was God's way of convincing the Jews. Incidentally, that's is what the seal is in Ephesians 1 and we will talk about it in another lesson. There are so many passages that are dispensational in the sense that they refer back to Acts 2 or they refer back to Acts 10. Acts 10 is significant. This was Gentiles being converted for the first time. Look again in Acts 15 where Peter said: "**Men and brethren, you know that a good while ago God chose among us, that by my mouth the Gentiles should hear the word of the gospel and believe. So God, who knows the heart, acknowledged them, by giving them the Holy Spirit just as He did to us...**" So, it not only convinced the Jews but it also put a seal of approval on the Gentiles and gave them confidence of His approval as well. God stamped His seal of approval on that conversion in no uncertain terms, by Holy Spirit baptism. Then those that heard Peter's explanation, (V18): **"When they heard these things they became silent; and they glorified God, saying, "Then God has also granted to the Gentiles repentance to life."**

THE SEAL OF APPROVAL

Turn with me to Eph. 1. The word seal is used in the bible to indicate that a thing is genuine or is a matter of protection and you know that. Paul begins to use some very general terms when he talks about spiritual blessings in Christ. Let's pick up at verse 4 and read through verse13; **"just as He chose us in Him before the foundation of the world, that we should be holy and without blame before Him in love, having predestined us to adoption as sons by Jesus Christ to Himself, according to the good pleasure of His will, to the praise of the glory of His grace, by which He has made us accepted in the Beloved. In Him we have redemption through His blood, the forgiveness of sins, according to the riches of His grace which He made to abound toward us in all wisdom and prudence, having made known to us the mystery of His will, according to His good pleasure which He purposed in Himself, that in the dispensation of the fullness of the times He might gather together in one all things in Christ, both which are in heaven and which are on earth-- in Him, in whom also we have obtained an inheritance, being predestined according to the purpose of Him who works all things according to the counsel of His will, that we** **[talking about the Jews] ** **who first trusted in Christ should be to the praise of His glory. In Him you** **[talking about the Gentiles] ** **also trusted, after you heard the word of truth, the gospel of your salvation; in whom also, having believed, you were sealed** **[stamped with approval] ** **with the Holy Spirit of promise**

My point is that Paul talks about the Jews who had before hoped in Christ and then he said you Gentiles are included as well. That word "seal" in that passage means that God stamped His approval on Gentile conversion and I am here to tell you that I am thankful that He did for I am a Gentile.

When did He do it if it was not in Acts 10? That is when He did it. Most assuredly, Cornelius received baptism of the Holy Spirit. Not for the same reason that the Apostles did but to show God's approval of Gentiles.

CHART #22	
HOW MANY BAPTISMS -- TODAY --	
TWO BAPTISMS AT PENTECOST .........A.D. 33 (Acts 1:5; 2:1-4,38)	
TWO BAPTISMS AT CAESAREA...... .... A.D. 41	
ONE BAPTISM............................ ......A.D. 62	
Holy Spirit Baptism	Water Baptism
1) Promise (Acts 1:5)	1) Commanded (Acts 10:48)
2) Administered only by Christ (Matt 3 :11)	2) Administered only by men (Matt 28 :18-20)
3) Ended before AD 62 (Eph. 4:5)	3) To the end of the world (Matt. 28:20)
"THERE IS --- ONE BAPTISM" Ephesians 4:5	

Just as the laying on of the apostles hands were for different purposes, to one "faith" to another "tongues" &etc. so the purpose of Holy Spirit baptism was for different purposes; it enabled the apostles to witness for Christ and provided them power that enabled them to establish His church, but to the Gentles is was a stamp of approval. There is no doubt about the fact that there were two baptisms on the day of Pentecost; Holy Spirit baptism and baptism in water for the remission of sins. There were two baptisms at Caesarea, Phillipi. In Acts 10:47, Peter commanded them to be baptized in water. So, there was water baptism and Holy Spirit baptism. But when Paul wrote to the Ephesians in Eph. 4:5 he said there was but one baptism. Now, no matter what you may think about what he means, he said there was only one baptism. I know that 1+1=2 and so do you. So, I submit to you that one of the baptisms had ceased and there can be no doubt about that. It was Holy Spirit baptism that ceased. Holy Spirit baptism was a promise,(Acts 1:5), it was not a command, you do not obey a promise. It was administered only by Christ, (Mat. 3:11). Water baptism is administered by men, (Mat. 28:18-20). Holy Spirit baptism ended before AD 62, (Eph. 4:5). Water baptism will continue until the end of time, (Mat.28:20). The baptism of Mat. 28:20 is, obviously, that one baptism Paul clearly states in Eph. 4. Why? Because it will continue until the end of the world. So, the one baptism today is water baptism as Jesus has directed in order that men might have their sins forgiven; to become a child of God through faith in Christ Jesus. Holy Spirit baptism has ceased. It was not promised to anyone today and it is not received by anyone today, contrary to the claims of men. But the lesson is yours. I trust this will help you in your study.

The End of Lesson Two

CHAPTER THREE

"Inspiration Of The Holy Spirit"

We are continuing our study of the Holy Spirit, His mission, work and how He accomplished that work. This will be a study about the Holy Spirit and the inspiration of the scriptures. We'll discuss how we got this book, the bible, but I'll not get into all the translations of the bible. That is not the point of interested in at this time.

I will, in the process of this lesson, show you from this book that it claims that the message of this book is a message from God. It was miraculously uncovered to the apostles and prophets. I stand before you and tell you that I believe with all my heart that through the providence of God he has protected that message. I have been studying with you from two different translations, the Kings James and the American Standard. If I am remembering correctly, 148 of the very best of Greek scholars were involved in these translations. We are talking about a message that was miraculously uncovered, made known, that has been recorded and I believe God has protected it through His providence.

The religious world, in general, will make the charge that if you don't believe that the Holy Spirit is working directly and performing miracles then you don't believe God is doing anything. They put you in a position of being a deist and in the next lesson we'll be studying more about this. They think that we are deist, that God got things all wound up and now he's sitting under a shade tree and just waiting and watching to see what will come to pass. Their charge is that we don't believe that God is doing anything. What seems so strange to me is that if people read their bible they surely must be aware of the fact that much of the things in the bible that describe what God did, he didn't do it with a miracle. He did it through his providence. That is a point we will consider further in the next lesson in our study. I certainly believe that God is still doing things and so do you. I believe that God acts through his providence. Now think with me, the bible teaches that Jesus is God, (Jno. 1:1-2). The bible teaches that the Holy Spirit is God, Acts 5 :24 and the Father is God. Therefore, the New Testament attributes deity to the Father, the Son and the Holy Spirit. I am firmly convinced that every time in the bible that you see the term "God", it is a comprehensive term. That term always involves the Father, the Son and the Holy Spirit unless there is something in the context to indicate otherwise. For instance, in Eph. 4 where you have the passage talking about one Lord, one Spirit and one God and Father. Here you have a distinction made. However, if that distinction is not there, the term "God" is comprehensive and always includes the Father, the Son and the Holy Spirit, the Godhead. If God acts through providence, and he does, who does that involve? It involves the Father, the Son and the Holy Spirit. I have no problem with that at all. Therefore, when people say that I don't believe that God is doing anything, that's not so.

The issue that I suggested to you in the first lesson is that it's not that the Holy Spirit does these things but how does he do it. Does he do this directly or does he do it indirectly through a medium. Therefore, in this lesson we are specifically concerned about the Holy Spirit and the scriptures, the word of God. I believe that through miracles this word, the New Testament, was revealed or uncovered and I believe I will be able to set that forth.

What does the Holy Spirit say to us about the scriptures, about this word? Is there some kind of relationship between the message of this New Testament and the Holy Spirit? Yes there is. I have used this repeatedly in the meeting thus far where Jesus in the presence of his ambassadors, the apostles, said to them, **"But the Comforter, which is the Holy Ghost whom the Father will send in my name, he shall teach you all things and bring all things to your remembrance whatsoever I said unto you".** We are going to look at the passages that tell us how he did it. We read in John 15:26 **"But when the Helper comes, whom I shall send to you from the Father, the Spirit of truth who proceeds from the Father, He will testify of Me."** Incidentally, this will be discussed at length in the next lesson when we study about the Holy Spirit and miracles and we'll bring special attention to the matter of tongues. In Jno.16:16, Jesus said: **"A little while, and ye behold me no more; and again a little while, and ye shall see me".** Therefore, the mission of the Holy Spirit according to the words of Jesus was that of revealing the divine truth! What does that word mean? We are going to look at it in a minute. If you think I am going to spend a lot of time in giving you dictionary meanings, I'm not. I am going to give you the meaning from this book on how that term "revealed" is used. Therefore, to reveal divine truth, teach all things, bring to remembrance all that Jesus taught, guide into all truth, reveal things to come and then confirm that truth and do so by bearing witness to it! This is revelation and confirmation! The Holy Spirit is involved, not any question about that and I could not consistently present a series of lessons about the Holy Spirit without talking to you about this.

There are two passages that I want to look at now and maybe bring them up again later. Turn with me to Mk. the 16:17-20. Jesus said: "**And these signs will follow those who believe: In My name they will cast out demons; they will speak with new tongues; "they will take up serpents; and if they drink anything deadly, it will by no means hurt them; they will lay hands on the sick, and they will recover." So then, after the Lord had spoken to them, He was received up into heaven, and sat down at the right hand of God. And they went out and preached everywhere, the Lord working with them and confirming the word through the accompanying signs. Amen.** " This passage is used by the Charismatic to try to prove that every believer must have these signs. We know better than that. We know that is not true. May I suggest to you that this passage simply indicates that signs would accompany them that believe and would confirm the word with signs that would follow. There is a reason for it and that as a consequence all that believed received a message and that message was confirmed by signs, It was verified or validated, not that every individual believer had to have these signs but these signs will accompany them that believe, they will be with them.

Let me show you another passage. This one is used many times by those who contend for a direct personal indwelling of the Holy Spirit, Acts 5 :32. Now, the apostles Peter had been in prison and he was questioned about his teaching and his preaching and he said: **"And we are witness of these things and so is the Holy Spirit whom God hath given to them that obey him"**. What is disturbing to me is that some of my brethren who can see the fallacy of the argument on Mk.16:17-20, and recognize that the passage doesn't teach that every individual believer would be able to perform signs and wonders but, they see this passage and think that God gave the Holy Spirit to everyone that obeyed him and therefore, when man obeys, God gives him the Holy Spirit. I believe these are companion passages and if a person can understand that Mk.16:17-20 is not teaching that every believer would perform signs and wonders and that the Holy Spirit would enable them to do so, they ought to be able to see that this passage is not teaching that everyone that obeys would receive the Holy Spirit. Peter say here that they were witnesses of these things. I just read the text a moment ago in Jno. 15:26 where Jesus said the Holy Spirit would bear witness to that truth that they presented. I submit to you that the message was validated, what they taught, and thus endorsed the results of that message.

Now think with me again. The Holy Spirit validated the message that they were teaching and as a consequence validated or endorsed the results of that teaching. What were the results of that teaching? It was Christianity! Those who became New Testament Christians! Therefore, Peter said, we can bare witness to the truth we have been teaching and the Holy Spirit bears witness to that as well and has been given to those who obey him. Been given how? As a witness. How did they witness that? It was by the signs and the wonders that were performed to witness or validate the message. Therefore, the Holy Spirit is involved as far as the truth is concerned, by validating the message.

With this before us we get into a definition of words. A word is a symbol of an idea; it's a vehicle of thought. If I want to communicate with you I do so through the medium of words. God selected that method of making his mind known. He could have used smoke signals if he wanted to but he didn't. He selected words. Therefore, the words that I will be using tonight, I need to define and make sure you understand how I'm using them.

If I use a word in one sense and you understand it in another, I'm guilty of ambiguity! An honest and good speaker doesn't do that. Let me repeat that. An honest and good speaker does not do that! If he is a good speaker, he wants to make sure that the audience understands how he is using the word. Also, if he's honest he wants to take extreme care that he is not misunderstood. This is why I want to define some of these terms.

CHART #23	
DEFINITION OF TERMS	
John 10:34-35 "---written in "…unto whom the "your law" …the scripture " word of God came" cannot be broken" IT FOLLOWS: THE LAW , THE WORD OF GOD, WAS <u>SCRIPTURE</u>	
Luke 24:44-45	
Jesus opened their mind that they might "understand the scriptures" ↔	**"things...written in the law of Moses, and in the prophets, and in psalms" (one way that the Jews had of dividing the law of Moses)**
IT FOLLOWS: THE LAW OF MOSES (WHICH WAS THE LAW OF GOD) WAS **<u>SCRIPTURE</u>**	

What do I mean when I say "by the scriptures"? The word scripture carries with it the idea of a script and fundamentally means something that is written. Does it mean anything and everything that is written? There is a sense in which that might be true but how is it used in the New Testament? That's like the word "baptism". People talk about a secondary meaning of the word and let me illustrate this point. I've had several debates with the non-class brethren and I've had to tolerate a statement that I made a long time ago. That's why for so many years I wouldn't write and may wish, later on, that I had started to do a little writing. I want to make sure when I put something down in print that it is correct. Something that is in writing becomes pretty definite and firm.

However, there is a debate book on classes and women teachers where our brethren took the position that we prophesy in a secondary way. Now you might find that in Webster's dictionary but they'll also tell you that you are baptized in a secondary way. I'm not willing to accept that. The bible tells me what prophesy involves. It involves inspiration and revelation, II Pet. 1:21 and I Cor. 14:32. You don't prophesy in a secondary way! Prophesy is a term that occurs in the New Testament and what the New Testament says about it is what I had better believe about it.

The same thing is true about the word "scripture". How is the word "scripture" used in the word of God? Let's see what the New Testament has to say about it. In Jno. 10: 34-35, Jesus answered them and said: **"Is it not written in your law, 'I said, "You are gods" '? If He called them gods, to whom the word of God came (and the Scripture cannot be broken),"** What is that passage saying? Does he not indicate it is written in your law and then further he said unto whom the word of God came and then he said the scripture can not be broken? Does he not in this instance identify the Law, the word of God, as scripture? He does, doesn't he? How does the bible use the word "scripture"? It uses it to refer to the word of God. That is how I am going to be using it also. Then again in Lk.24 : 44 - 45, he said unto them: ***"These are the words which I spoke to you while I was still with you, that all things must be fulfilled which were written in the Law of Moses and the Prophets and the Psalms concerning Me." And He opened their understanding, that they might comprehend the Scriptures."*** Did you know that this is one of the passages that is used in order to justify instrumental music? I know this lesson is not on instrumental music but I mention this since I have this passage before you. They will cite the book of Psalms about instrumental music. You say, well no, that was the Old Testament and they say no, Jesus said it was the Law, the Psalms, and the Prophets. The first time I heard that explained properly I was attending Southwestern Baptist Seminary in Fort Worth Texas. They knew what that was talking about. They knew there were three ways the Jews divided the Old Testament. They know the Psalms are part of the Old Testament and I can show you numerous passages in the New

Testament where the book of Psalms is quoted and is said of the Jews, it's your Law. But, those folks at Southwestern knew that. It was written of the Law of Moses and the Prophets and the Psalms concerning me. Then he open their minds to an understanding of the scriptures.

CHART #24

DEFINITION: **"INSPIRATION"** THE WORD IS DEFINED TO MEAN "GOD BREATHED"	"By the word of Jehovah were the heavens made, And all the host of them by the breath of his mouth." PSALMS 33:6

THE ORIGINAL IS A COMBINATION OF 2 WORDS:
One Meaning **GOD**, The Other Meaning **BREATHED**
Made The Heavens By:
"Word of the Lord" "Breath of His mouth"
Men of old were "MOVED" by the Holy Spirit
"Every scripture is inspired of god"---2 Tim. 3:16-17

"GOD-BREATHED

Note, if you will. Jesus opened their minds that they might understand the scriptures. Well, what has he identified as scriptures? It was things written in the Law of Moses and of the Prophets and of the Psalms; one way the Jews had of dividing the Law of Moses. It followed therefore that the Law of Moses, which was the Law of God, was scripture. The Adventist denies that but this passage says that it is. How am I using the word scripture? I'm using it just the way it is used here! Every scripture is inspired of God! We will look at this more in just a little while. Therefore, by the word "scripture", the bible means the word of God and that is how I am using it in our lesson. You will know then that when I talk about scripture I'm talking about the word of God.

Now, about the word "inspiration". The modernist doesn't believe the same about inspiration that you and I do. I attended school for a little while at TCU. They claim to be Christian but they are everything but that. Wait a minute, some of the liberal arts teachers had a little religion but in the religion department they didn't have any. I promise you they didn't. They would say, "Well certainly we believe in the inspiration of the scriptures" but what they meant was that scripture was inspired kind of like the writings of Shakespeare were inspired. They meant that the writers were merely influence, not directed. Therefore, when the modernist tells you he believes in the inspiration of the scriptures, keep in mind that this is what he means. He does not believe what the word of God has to say about it. In Psa. 33 : 6, the Lord says: **"By the word of the LORD the heavens were made, And all the host of them by the breath of His mouth."** That is one of the passages that helps explain Heb. 11:3. I don't know if you have noticed that or not but the writer says by faith we understand that the world was framed by the word of God. W.E. Vine says that has to do with intellect. How do we understand that the world was framed by the word of God? This and other passages say that it was. This is how we understand it. "Faith comes by hearing and hearing by the word of God."(Romans 10:17). The word is defined to mean God breathed. That is what the word literally means. Inspiration is the combination of two words, one meaning God and the other meaning breathed. This verse in Psalms 33, verse 6, said by the word of the Lord the heavens were made but he made them by the breath of his mouth. Therefore, the definition of that term fits exactly what that passage has to say. In II Pet. 1:20, 21: **"knowing this first, that no prophecy of Scripture is of any private interpretation, for prophecy never came by the will of man, but holy men of God spoke as they were moved by the Holy Spirit."** That's a combination of two terms, a verb and a preposition which means "man's own loosening". It didn't originate with man. This is used many times to say you don't have the right to study and interpret the scriptures, the preacher or the priest has to do that for you. That's not what Peter is saying. Not of man's own unloosening and the next passage tells you why. He says, **"For the prophecy came not in old time by the will of man"**. It didn't originate with man but men; holy men of God spoke as the Holy Spirit moved them. I submit to you then that is what Peter declared. Peter declared that holy men of God were moved, carried on or borne along by the Holy Spirit. Therefore, the matter of a God breathed message. This is why I said to you that every scripture is inspired of God, II Tim. 3:16 - 17,). This is a passage that says a lot to me, it means a lot to me and it should to you. This passage tells we what the tools are that we have to do our work. In that passage Paul has said to Timothy, **"Every scripture inspired of God is profitable for doctrine, correction, instruction of righteousness that the man of God may be complete".** The man of God in this instance is talking about the preacher. You won't find it anywhere in the New Testament except in the books of First and Second Timothy. Primarily, that passage is saying that the scriptures, the word of God, is the information that a preacher needs to do his work of preaching. This is the information that he must have. As one preacher said, "All of the commentaries have a lot of light shed on them by the scriptures". That is right. I have a lot of books in my library, I use them but I'll not understand the truth without referring to the scriptures. The scriptures are the source that I must go to. That is what Paul is saying. Certainly, the passage indicates that the word of God furnishes every man with all the information that he needs to live right but that is not the primary lesson. The primary lesson is to instruct Timothy that he has the tools necessary to do his job. This is why Paul said, **"Preach the word, be urgent in season, out of season, reprove, rebuke and exhort with all long suffering".** Therefore, the scriptures, the God breathed message, that's the meaning of inspiration.

One other term that I would like to define is the word "revelation" and then we will look at some passages. What does the word "revelation" mean? In Mat. 10: 26 we have a contrast. I'll touch on this subject only briefly, as a more lengthy examination will follow in another lesson. You have numerous contrasts in the New Testament. Contrasts are opposites. Isaac B. Grubbs, in his book on Biblical Hermeneutics, says there are two fundamental principles upon which all bible interpretation rests and I agree with him. One of them is the basic Law of Harmony that presupposes the unity or harmony of truth. Therefore, any interpretation or application of one passage that conflicts with another must be rejected. This is why you must look at all the facts in the case. The second one has to do with the Law of Opposition or the Law of Contrast.

He goes on in his book and points out the fact that you can learn what is in the writers' mind by looking at the opposite of that which you read. I will give you a "for instance". In Rom. 6 : 23 where the writer said, **"the wages of sin are death, but the free gift of God is life eternal".** Men have played on the phrase "free gift" haven't they? They will make it mean everything imaginable. It's whatever they want it to mean. What is the opposite of "free gift" here? It's "wages of sin" because these are opposites being presented. What does the word "wage" mean? It simply means something that man deserves. What does "free gift" mean? It means something that he doesn't deserve. That is basically what "free gift" means and for men to play on it and make it mean what they want it to mean is a mistake.

Chart #25
DEFINION: "REVEALED" (Mat. 10:26)
"Fear them not therefore: for there is nothing covered, that shall not be revealed; and hid, that shall not be known." NOTE TERMS: *COVERED = HID *REVEALED = KNOWN "REVEALED": *Making KNOWN the UNKNOWN *UNCOVERING the HIDDEN
MAKING KNOW WHATIS HIDDEN

Therefore, what I'm going to do with this word "reveal" is to look at the text and see how it is used. Watch it if you will. Jesus said in Mat. 10:26, **"Fear them not therefore; for there is nothing covered, that shall not be revealed; and hid, that shall not be known".** Here you have opposites. What is the opposite of covered? It's uncovered. What is the term that is used? It's revealed! Therefore, the opposite of covered is uncovered and the term "revealed" is used in that opposition. The term "covered" means that which is "hid" and "reveal" means that which is "known". You can spend an hour if you wanted to reading definitions about the word reveal and you are not going to come up with a better definition than that because that's exactly what the term means. It means making known the unknown.

CHART #26
RECEIVED BY REVELATION (Gal. 1:11-12)
"For I make known to you, brethren, as touching the gospel which was preached by me, that it is not after man. For neither did I receive it from man, nor was I taught it, but {it came to me} through revelation of Jesus Christ.."   **THE GOSPEL PREACHED BY PAUL**   **1) NOT AFTER MAN (didn't originate with man)**   **2) NOT RECEIVED FROM MAN (not an indirect message)**   **3) NOT TAUGHT IT (not instructed)**   **4) CAME THRU REVELATION OF JESUS CHRIST**
MAKE KNOWN DIRECTLY

With this in mind let's look at some passages that have to do with our subject. Turn to Galatians the first chapter and verse 11 where Paul said, **"I certify"** (make known) **"you, brethren, that the gospel which was preached of me is not after man".** What does he mean? He is talking about the origin of the gospel; it's not after men. Verse 12 says: **"For I neither received it of man, neither was I taught it, but by the revelation of Jesus Christ"**. He goes on and says in verse 17 that he did not go up to Jerusalem to them that were apostles before him but went into Arabia and returned again unto Damascus. What Paul admits is that the other apostles had not taught him. Therefore, Paul says that the gospel he preached was not from man, it did not originate with man. We have read that also in II Pet. 1.

Secondly, it was not received from man nor was it an indirect message. He has denied that the other apostles taught him anything. The independence of his apostleship is obviously involved at least in the discussion at this instance. Paul said it came to him through "revelation" of Jesus Christ. It was made known directly. This passage in Mat. 10:26 simply indicates that here was something that was "made known". Keep this in mind as we begin to examine this from other text.

Chart #27
--- Ephesians 3:3-5 ---
NOTE THESE CONCLUSIONS: 1) By **Revelation** The **Mystery** (Previously Undisclosed) Was Made **Known** To Paul 2) That Which Was **Made Known** To Paul He Wrote. 3) What Paul **Wrote**, The Ephesians Could **Understand** When They Read It. 4) This **Mystery** Made Known To Paul Had Not Been Taught. 5) The Method Of Making This Mystery Known Was By **Revelation Of The Spirit** Through Apostles & Prophets. **HENCE:** The Holy Spirit revealed the Gospel of Christ to the Apostles & Prophets, thus enabling them to write down the message
Revelation-Words-Read-Perceive

In Eph. 3:1 Paul writes: "For this reason I, Paul, the prisoner of Jesus Christ for you Gentiles--if indeed you have heard of the dispensation of the grace of God which was given to me for you, how that by revelation He made known to me the mystery (as I wrote before in a few words," This text tells us what the word revelation means doesn't it? "How that by revelation he made known unto me the mystery". There are those that say the gospel is mysterious. That's not what Paul is saying. They would have you believe that the gospel of Christ is mysterious and incomprehensible; that you cannot read it and understand it. They say you have to have some direct event or help from the Holy Spirit in order to understand the word of God because it is mysterious. This is not what this passage says, but the contrary. The passage says, "How was made known unto me the mystery". When you look at the text it becomes evident that Paul said it was made known unto him. He understood the mystery. He then confirms what I have been saying to you, he said, "As I wrote before in few words". Words were selected as a means or medium of communication. This is the first thing that I would suggest to you, that the writer said, that this message was made known unto him, he wrote it. Let's read on in Verse 4: "by which, when you read, you may understand my knowledge in the mystery of Christ)," Paul said he understood it, it was made known unto him, he wrote it and he said when we read it we can perceive it. What does perceive mean? It means you can understand it. The next verse defines the word mystery for us. The word mystery simply means something that has not, prior to this time, been made known. It would be a good project to search your New Testament and find everywhere the word "mystery" occurs in connection with the gospel of Christ and see if there is not something in the immediate context that tells you that you are able to understand it. Therefore, in verse 5 he said: "which in other ages was not made known to the sons of men, as it has now been revealed by the Spirit to His holy apostles and prophets:" This was something that prior to that time had not been made known but now has been revealed, uncovered or made known unto his Holy apostles and prophets through the Spirit. Several years ago in Quincy, Louisiana I was moderating for a friend of mine in a debate with a Charismatic preacher. This Charismatic preacher stood up and made this statement that so many of them do, he said: "Now this man thinks that Holy Spirit baptism just enabled the apostles to write the New Testament". He also said, "It becomes evident to everyone that there were some who wrote the New Testament who weren't apostles. How about that"? (He was going to call him out). He turned to me and said, "How about that?" And I said, "Prophets".

In our next lesson we'll learn that prophecy was one of the gifts that the apostles were able to impart; the gift of prophecy. The prophets were also able to reveal, uncover, and make known the will of God. That is what this passage is saying; **"which in other ages was not made known to the sons of men, as it has now been revealed by the Spirit to His holy apostles and prophets:"** The mystery was made known, Paul wrote it, and when the Ephesians read it they could understand it. If they could understand it when they read it, I can understand it when I read it. I may not, but I can! You may not but you are able to! Also, this passage says that what was made known to the Apostle Paul was not made known to previous generations. Therefore, making this message known was by revelation of the Spirit. The Spirit is involved in this revealing or uncovering and made known through the apostle and prophets. That is what the passage says, doesn't it? Therefore, I submit to you that the Holy Spirit revealed the gospel of Christ to the apostles and prophets and thus enabling them to write down the message! Revelation, words, read and perceive that passage says.

MYSTERY REVEALED

Chart #28
MYSTERY REVEALED (Part 1 of 2)
1) The Message That Paul Preached Reflected Wisdom -- Even God's (V. 6) 2) This Wisdom Spoken In "A Mystery" (V. 7) "Something That Had Not Been Known" The Context Makes This Clear 3) This Mystery Was Hidden In The Mind Of God Before the World, Or Ages (V. 7) 4) This Mystery Was Unknown By Rulers (V. 8) 5) To This Agrees The Words Of Isaiah (V. 9) This Message Not Detected by Human Eye or Ear Neither Had It Entered Man's Heart or Mind Man Never Saw It, Heard It, or Thought of It 6) That Which Was Hidden (That Which Man Never Saw, Heard Or Thought Of) Was Revealed Through The Spirit (V. 10)
I Cor. 2:6-9

If you would turn with me to I Corinthians 2. May I suggest to you that the Apostle Paul had talked about his preaching at Corinth but he hadn't tried to impress them with Paul, what Paul thought; he didn't try to impress them with words of man's wisdom. Also, for fear that they might think that what he taught and what he preached was not wisdom he said in verse 6: **"However, we speak wisdom among those who are mature, yet not the wisdom of this age, nor of the rulers of this age, who are coming to nothing. But we speak the wisdom of God in a mystery, the hidden wisdom which God ordained before the ages for our glory,"** Now there's that term "mystery" again. Same writer now and using the same terms. Look at what he says in the rest of that sentence, **"even the hidden wisdom that God ordained".** I pause now and ask you, where was that hidden? It was hidden in the mind of God. Mark that in your mind. This is the only passage that I know about in the New Testament that precisely tells you how God made his mind known to man. That is like Jam. 1 :13 - 15; the only passage that I know of in the scriptures that gives you the birth of sin. When did sin occur? Was it at the point of desire or was it at the point of action? I'm amazed brethren! The word lust means desire, the context will tell you whether it's bad or not. Therefore, this passage says that man is tempted by his own lust, only that, and enticed and then lust when it is <u>conceived</u> brings forth sin. There's the birth of sin just like this passage identifies how God made his mysteries known to man. Read on with me then: **"But we speak the wisdom of God in a mystery, the hidden wisdom which God ordained before the ages for our glory, ... which none of the princes of this world knew".** Man didn't know it. It was a mystery. Had they known it they would not have crucified the Lord of glory. Next he cites an Old Testament passage that corroborates this, verse 9: **"But as it is written: "Eye has not seen, nor ear heard, nor have entered into the heart of man the things which God has prepared for those who love Him."**

I attended a funeral service a few weeks ago where the preacher read this passage and applied it to heaven. It no more applies to heaven than it does to baptism, brethren. That is a total misrepresentation, misapplication of the scriptures. How you get heaven in the context when it tells about how God revealed His mind to the mind of man is difficult for me to see. This fits with the immediate context. What is he talking about? He's talking about the revelation of his mind. Therefore, he points out that the eye didn't see it, man didn't see it, he didn't hear it and he didn't think about it. **"Whatsoever things that God prepared for them that love him".** What is he talking about? He is talking about that which was a mystery that the rulers of this world had not known, that was hidden in the mind of God, that's the gospel he is talking about!

Chart #29
MYSTERY REVEALED (Part 2 Of 2)
7) A Simple Illustration In Verses 11&12 a) No One Knows What is in Man's Mind -- Except that Man's Spirit b) Just So, No One Knew the Mind of God -- Except the Spirit of God 8) Obvious Conclusion: Paul Declared that he & others " **Received the Spirit of God,**" That they "**MIGHT KNOW THE THINGS OF GOD"** 9) They were able to speak this message, that had been a mystery hidden in the mind of God 10) They spoke this message in words which the Holy Spirit taught
I Cor. 2:10-13

Look at the next verse. Verse 10, "**But unto us God revealed them**". What did he reveal? Those things which eye saw not and ear heard not, which entered not into the heart of man. Here's one of those passages that you have difficulty with if you don't recognize that context involves the remote context as well as the immediate. Who is the "us" he is talking about? The immediate context doesn't tell you. You see context, ladies and gentlemen, involves a statement. It involves the immediate; that which precedes the statement and that which follows it; and it involves all other related truths. I don't know any subject that the Lord exhausts the first time it is mentioned do you? Therefore, we have to look at all the facts in the case. This passage does not identify whom it is talking about but Eph. 3 does. It's talking about the same things; it's talking about the revelation of the mind of God; it's talking about that which is made known by the Holy Spirit. That's what this is talking about and therefore the "us" is identified in Eph. 3. Who were they? The "us" were the apostles and prophets. They were the ones who by inspiration were able to reveal the will of God. This is what it is talking about and Eph. 3 shows it. "**But unto us God revealed them through the Spirit**". That's the subject we are talking about. The Holy Spirit uncovered and made these things known. **"For the Spirit searches all things, yea the deep things of God"**. Verse 11 is a simple illustration and simply declares who among men knows the things of a man save the spirit of man, which is in him. I don't know what's in your mind because I don't have your spirit. If I had your spirit I would know what is in your mind. Now, watch his application, "Even so the things of God none know save the Spirit of God". Just as the spirit of man knows what is in the mind of that man, he says the Spirit of God knows what is in the mind of God. That's why I said to you that the message was hidden in the mind of God. I don't take any serious exception to the fact that you can't judge a man's motives but I still think that you have to consider that Jesus said in Mat. 7, **"by their fruits you shall know them".** You have to put that into context as well. He simply says you don't know what's in the mind of men if you don't have his spirit. Now whenever he speaks and whenever he acts he reveals some things about himself **for "Out of the abundance of the heart the mouth speaks"**. Therefore, there are other passages involved in this that we need to consider. He says: **"Even so the things of God none know save the Spirit of God", but watch what else he says. "For we received not the spirit of the world but the spirit which is from God that we might know the things freely given us of God".** This tells you how God made his mind known to man. By miracles, I don't have any doubt about it. I don't have any doubt that this was miraculous. The Holy Spirit enabled the apostles and prophets to make known, uncover, and reveal the mind of God. They were able to write it and Eph. 3 said so. Now then, look at verse 13: **"These things we also speak, not in words which man's wisdom teaches but which the Holy Spirit teaches, comparing spiritual things with spiritual."** The Modernist will tell us that the Holy Spirit just revealed the thought and these men used their own words to express that thought and maybe they didn't express the proper thoughts. I can still see the professor when he would explain that and he would say, "he just revealed the thought to them" and you could see it written all over him that they weren't as smart as he was. They didn't have the background that he did and maybe they did not use the proper words to describe their thoughts. That is infidelity and that's all you can make of it. This is what those professionals are subjecting to a lot of your children.

Summary

Reading now in verse 12: **"Now we have received, not the spirit of the world, but the spirit which is of God; that we might know the things**

that are freely given to us of God" and verse 13, "Which things also we speak, not in the words which man's wisdom teach, but which the Holy Ghost teaches ; combining spiritual things with spiritual words". Therefore, you have thoughts and words in revelation. That is what the passage says and I submit to you that the New Testament makes it perfectly clear that this mystery has been revealed. This is going to confirm what I've gone through the text and looked at with you. Note if you will the message that Paul preached reflected wisdom; it reflected God's wisdom, that's what it said in verse 6. It was something that before had not been made known. It was hidden in the mind of God before the world came into existence, verse 7. This message was unknown by rulers, verse 8, and spoken of by Isaiah, verse 9. This message was not detected by human eye or ear; neither had it been in man's heart or mind and man never saw it; heard it or thought of it. This is the message that Paul is talking about. It was revealed through the Spirit, verse 10. That is what these passages say, verses 6 through 9.

I trust you get the force of what this is teaching. You see, it's a mistake to take a passage out of its context and make it mean what you want it to mean. We see that verse 11 has something to do with what he is talking about. He was talking about the wisdom of God. This wisdom of God was hidden in the mind of God and that it has now been revealed. That illustration is telling you how he revealed it. Let's go over it again. Who among men knows the things of a man save the spirit of the man that is in him, even so the things of God. Now, if I knew or had your spirit or if I had God's Spirit I would know what you or He has in mind. The writer says the same thing about the mind of God. No one knows the mind of God save the Spirit of God. To me that's just as plain as the nose on my face. It was a mystery hidden in the mind of God and they spoke this message in words, which the Holy Spirit taught, verse 13. These passages show how that God made his mind known to man. I don't think that men understand that Jesus did not write his last will and testament. The only thing that he wrote was something on the ground when the woman was taken in adultery. He selected his ambassadors, the apostles, and they were able to impart the gift of prophecy.

Chart #30

MISSION OF THE HOLY SPIRIT

Jno. 14:26; 15:26; 16:12-13

I. REVEAL DIVINE THRUTH

1. "Teach all things"

2. "Bring to remembrance all Jesus had taught"

3. "Reveal things to come"

II. CONFIRM TRUTH

1. "Bear witness"

NOTE:

TRUTH ABOUT WHAT TO DO TO BE SAVED, NOW AND ETERNALLY!

The Holy Spirit enabled the apostles and prophets to make known the mind of God. Jesus promised them that He would send a Helper, the Spirit of truth to help them in preaching the gospel message:

(Jno. 14:26): **"But the Helper, the Holy Spirit, whom the Father will send in My name, He will teach you all things, and bring to your remembrance all things that I said to you."**

(Jno. 15:26): **"But when the Helper comes, whom I shall send to you from the Father, the Spirit of truth who proceeds from the Father, He will testify of Me.**

(Jno. 16:12-13): **"I still have many things to say to you, but you cannot bear them now. However, when He, the Spirit of truth, has come, He will guide you into all truth; for He will not speak on His own authority, but whatever He hears He will speak; and He will tell you things to come.** So, the mission of the Holy Spirit was to **"reveal divine truth"**; "Teach all things"; "Bring to remembrance of His apostles all He had taught them"; and to "Reveal things to come". In addition to that, the Holy Spirit would enable them to "Bear witness" and to verify the message as well as the messenger.

A CONTRAST IN WALK

That message for a period of time, just how long I don't know, was in men, earthen vessels, and there were signs and wonders to validate that message. How else could we know they were teaching the truth? This message was in men, it was oral. Just how long before men started writing it I don't know. You know just as I do that there was a period of time when some of it was written and some was oral. Paul declared that in II Thes. 2 :15: **"Therefore, brethren, stand fast and hold the traditions which you were taught, whether by word or our epistle."** There are no prophets today except for false prophets. Therefore, I submit to you that the word of God for a period of time was oral, it was in men. For a period of time some of it was oral and some of it was written. It now is in the book, it is written down. The Roman Catholic Church will tell you that the "voice" of the church takes precedence. They say the Bible is true but does not contain all the truth and the Church and Pope are authorized to supplement and even over rule the scriptures. They claim the Church at Rome was established by Peter and that Peter left the reigns of sovereignty over the church to the Pope who sits in the chair of Peter, having all of his rights, powers and privileges. However, we see that the Holy Spirit led the apostles and prophets into all truth and enabled them to write it down so that we might know what the "perfect will of God is". History supplies ample proof that the Catholic claim is false and for several hundred years they were without such powers and authority among the Churches of Christ. The early church fathers denied any bishop who tried to rule over them.

There are no prophets today except for false prophets. Therefore, I submit to you that the word of God for a period of time was oral, it was in men. For a period of time some of it was oral and some of it was written. It now is in the book, it is written down. The Roman Catholic Church will tell you that the "voice" of the church takes precedence. They say the Bible is true but does not contain all the truth and the Church and Pope are authorized to supplement and even over rule the scriptures.

They claim the Church at Rome was established by Peter and that Peter left the reigns of sovereignty over the church to the Pope who sits in the chair of Peter, having all of his rights, powers and privileges. However, we see that the Holy Spirit led the apostles and prophets into all truth and enabled them to write it down so that we might know what the "perfect will of God is".

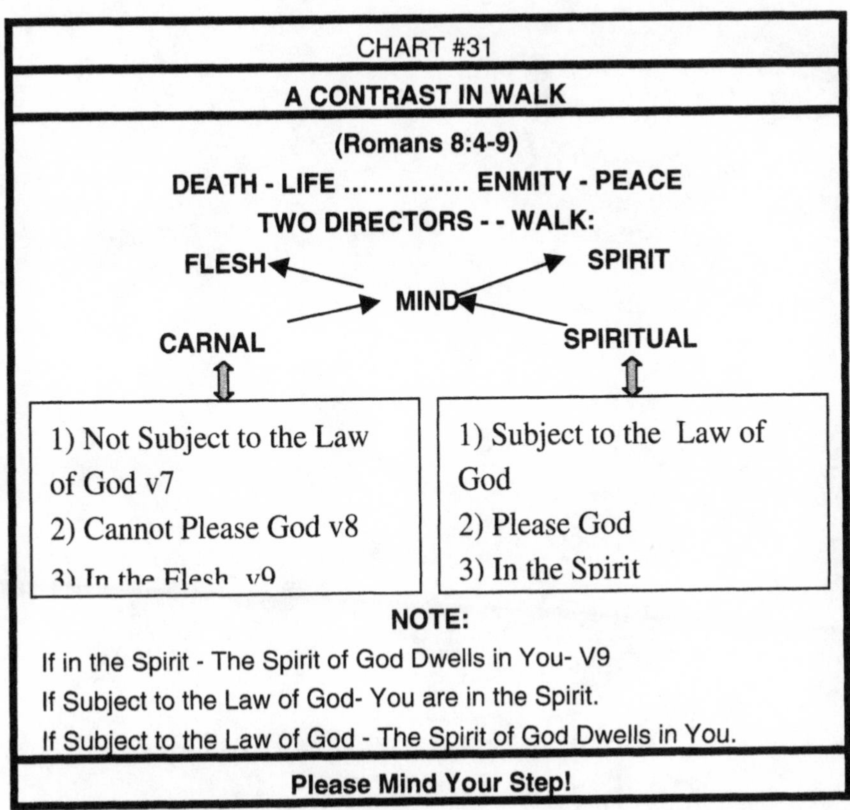

History supplies ample proof that the Catholic claim is false and for several hundred years they were without such powers and authority among the Churches of Christ. The early church fathers denied any bishop who tried to rule over them.

I believe I have successfully shown that the New Testament teaches that the mind of God was uncovered, revealed, made known and this was done miraculously by the Holy Spirit. I believe with all of my heart that through the Providence of God it has been protected. I believe we have an accurate record. I believe man can learn the truth, he can know what to do to be saved, he can know what to do to worship the Lord in the way that is acceptable to Him.

The End of Lesson Three

CHAPTER FOUR

"Signs and Wonders"

Our lesson tonight is on the matter of signs and wonders (miracles); their purpose; to whom they were promised and their duration. But before we begin that lesson, I have some questions on last nights lesson concerning Holy Spirit baptism. I will answer these questions and then move into our lesson for tonight.

Question: Did Jesus receive it or was He the administrator of it?
My answer is: He was the administrator of it. I read that in Jno. 1:33-34: **"And I knew him not: but he that sent me to baptize in water, he said unto me, Upon whomsoever thou shalt see the Spirit descending, and abiding upon him, the same is he that baptizeth in the Holy Spirit. And I have seen, and have borne witness that this is the Son of God."** So, I don't have to guess about that, do I? John testifies to the same thing in Mat. 3:11: **"I indeed baptize you in water unto repentance: but he that cometh after me is mightier than I, whose shoes I am not worthy to bear: he shall baptize you in the Holy Spirit and {in} fire:"**

Next Question: What is the difference in being baptized by the Holy Spirit and being filled with the Holy Spirit? My Answer: Sometimes these two terms are synonymous, I come to realize that to be the case in Acts 2:1-4; where we read: **"And when the day of Pentecost was now come, they were all together in one place. And suddenly there came from heaven a sound as of the rushing of a mighty wind, and it filled all the house where they were sitting. And there appeared unto them tongues parting asunder, like as of fire; and it sat upon each one of them. And they were all filled with the Holy Spirit, and began to speak with other tongues, as the Spirit gave them utterance."** However, it does not follow that because, in that instance, the Holy Spirit baptism is referred to as being "filled with the Spirit" that every time some one is said to be filled with the Spirit it means Holy Spirit baptism. I call your attention to Lk. 1:15; 1: 41 and 1:67 speaking of John the Baptist: **"For he shall be great in the sight of the Lord, and he shall drink no wine nor strong drink; and he shall be filled with the Holy Spirit,**

even from his mother's womb." **And in verse 41:"And it came to pass, when Elisabeth heard the salutation of Mary, the babe leaped in her womb; and Elisabeth was filled with the Holy Spirit;"** And in verse 67: **"And his father Zacharias was filled with the Holy Spirit, and prophesied, saying,..."** The record says that John was filled with the Holy Spirit from his mothers womb and this was before Holy Spirit Baptism was promised. (Mat. 3:11), Elizabeth was filled by the Holy Spirit and Zacharias was filled with the Holy Spirit all before Holy Spirit Baptism was received (Acts 2). Not only is that the case but in Eph. 5:18-19 where the writer said be filled with the Spirit: **"And be not drunken with wine, wherein is riot, but be filled with the Spirit; speaking one to another in psalms and hymns and spiritual songs, singing and making melody with your heart to the Lord;"** In Col. 3:16. I believe this is a parallel passage to Eph. 5, the writer said: **"Let the word of Christ dwell in you richly; in all wisdom teaching and admonishing one another with psalms {and} hymns {and} spiritual songs, singing with grace in your hearts unto God."** My point is this, these passages are teaching the same thing. In this instance, being filled with the Spirit and let the word of Christ dwell in you richly, are synonymous expressions.

One other point before we get into our lesson for the night. When the apostles were baptized with the Holy Spirit, (Acts 2:1-4) , it was said of them, that they were filled with the Holy Spirit. But at some time later in Acts 4:31, the record says: **"And when they had prayed, the place was shaken wherein they were gathered together; and they were all filled with the Holy Spirit, and they spake the word of God with boldness."** So they were not baptized by the Holy Spirit twice. Sometimes being filled with the Holy Spirit means being baptized by the Holy Spirit but it does not follow that it always means baptism by the Holy Spirit.

SIGNS AND MIRACLES

Last night we talked about inspiration and the Holy Spirit. I endeavored to impress upon you the fact that God miraculously revealed His mind to man, that is, the message that man was intended to receive, the Gospel of Christ. In Hebrews the second chapter, after he indicated that God speaks to us in this age through His son in the first chapter, the writer says that He exalted him over the Angels; Angels worship him; Angels serve Him. In the second chapter then, he says therefore, in view of the greatness of the Son we ought to pay greater heed to His word: **"Therefore we ought to give the more earnest heed to the things that were heard, lest haply we drift away {from them}. For if the word spoken through angels proved stedfast, and every transgression and disobedience received a just recompense of reward; how shall we escape, if we neglect so great a salvation? which having at the first been spoken through the Lord, was confirmed unto us by them that heard; God also bearing witness with them, both by signs and wonders, and by manifold powers, and by gifts of the Holy Spirit, according to his own will."** So, we have the subject of our study mentioned in this text. I believe the Hebrew letter, fundamentally, is an effort on the part of the writer to show that the choice that God made to address the world through His Son was a good one. He exalts him above angels and then points out that angels who are not as great yet when God spoke through them we had to respect what they revealed. How much more then when He speaks through His Son who is greater than they. In other words, he takes the lower and the higher; The lower are the angels and the word spoken through them God demanded that we respect it. The higher is the Son and thus man must pay attention to the Son. After that he makes a comparison between Christ and Moses; between Christianity and Judaism. And after he spent no little time showing the greatness of Christianity over Judaism and Christ over Moses he said in 10:28-29: **"A man that hath set at nought Moses law dieth without compassion on {the word of} two or three witnesses: of how much sorer punishment, think ye, shall he be judged worthy, who hath trodden under foot the Son of God, and hath counted the blood of the covenant wherewith he was sanctified an unholy thing, and hath done despite unto the Spirit of grace?"** The greater and the lesser is illustrated again. So the Hebrew letter is showing that the choice to address the world through His Son was a good one. A good choice that we must pay attention to. The passage says that this great salvation was spoken through the Lord and it was confirmed. That just simply indicates that there was sufficient evidence to cause people to recognize that this was in fact the truth. It was confirmed to us by them that heard; by signs and wonders; by manifold powers; and gifts (distribution is what the word literally means) of the Holy Spirit. He said this was by the will of the Holy Spirit.

In I Cor. 12, Paul identified these gifts of the Holy Spirit and indicates that the Holy Spirit was indeed a giver of gifts. In verse 8 he says: **"For to one is given through the Spirit the word of wisdom; and to another the word of knowledge, according to the same Spirit: to another faith, in the same Spirit; and to another gifts of healings, in the one Spirit; and to another workings of miracles; and to another prophecy; and to another discernings of spirits; to another {divers} kinds of tongues; and to another the interpretation of tongues: but all these worketh the one and the same Spirit, dividing to each one severally even as he will.** So, here you have a biblical definition of what it means when the Holy Spirit is said to do something in or by the Holy Spirit; its through or according to His will. There is not any question then that the passage indicates that the Holy Spirit is responsible for the signs, wonders and gifts and it was according to His own distribution. Ladies and gentlemen, there has never been a time in the history of the world that there has not been false miracle workers. They have been around for a long time and they are still around. In Prove. 25:14 we read where Solomon says: **"{As} clouds and wind without rain, {So is} he that boasteth himself of his gifts falsely."** That just simply says they promise what they cannot produce. In Acts the 8th Chapter, Simon the sorcerer was precisely that; A false miracle worker and he bewitched the people and they all gave heed saying "he is the great power of God" . But he wasn't, he was a fake. In Mat. 24, Jesus said there would be false prophets that would arise and they would show great wonders. In II The. 2:9, Paul talks about them being "after the working of Satan with lying signs, powers and wonders".

In Mat. 7, Jesus points out that there would be those who would say "Lord, did we not cast out demons and did we not do many mighty works in thy name" and so on. But Jesus will answer them "I will say to them, depart from me you workers of inequity, I never knew you" . So they have always been around and they are around today.

Chart #32
FALSE MIRACLE WORKERS
1. Prov. 25:14 "... Boasteth himself of a false gift is like clouds and wind without rain."   2. Acts 8:9-11 Simon bewitched the people – they all gave heed saying – great power of God.   3. Mat. 24:24 False prophets show great wonders   4. II Thes. 2:9 After the working of Satan with power, signs and lying wonders.   5. Mat. 7:22,23 Many say - cast out demons. Jesus will say "I never knew you. Depart from me ..."
Try False Claimers. (1 Jno. 4:1)

The first debate that I engaged in was on this subject as well as that of the Godhead. The man I was meeting asked me the question: "Are there any signs being performed today"? I answered him by reading to him II Thes. 2:8-9; **"And then shall be revealed the lawless one, whom the Lord Jesus shall slay with the breath of his mouth, and bring to nought by the manifestation of his coming; {even he}, whose coming is according to the working of Satan with all power and signs and lying wonders,".** Then I said, those kind are still around, they've been around for a long time.

DEFINITIONS OF SIGNS

What is a sign anyhow, what does the word mean. We'll try to define "signs" and we'll try to properly define what a miracle is. A sign is defined to be: "Of miraculous acts, as a token of divine authority and power." In other words a miraculous act that indicates that divine authority and divine power is behind that act. It Attests to the validity of a person or action. It gives assurance of truth. (Heb. 2:4).

Do you remember in Exodus the 4th chapter concerning Moses, (Ex. 4:1-5) when the Lord was sending him back into Egypt, he was reluctant to go saying they will not believe me. The Lord said what's that in your hand? It was a rod and when he cast it down it became a serpent and when he picked it up it became a rod again.

Chart #33
DEFINITIONS OF SIGNS
Of miraculous acts, as a token of divine authority and power. NOTE: Attests to the validity of a person or action. Give assurance of truth. Heb 2:4. **ILLUSTRATION:** Ex. 4:1-5 Signs by Moses to validate Moses and his message. Acts 8:6 Signs done by Philip To Validate Philip and his message. "Gave heed to the things SPOKEN by Philip, when they HEARD, and SAW the signs which he did"

There were several miracles that Moses was able to perform. What was the purpose of them? Obviously, it was to validate Moses, proving that God had sent him and to prove that the message he spoke unto them was to be accepted. That was the purpose of miracles back then. In Acts the 8th chapter, signs were given by Philip to validate Philip and his message. They didn't have the written New Testament but he could perform those signs and the record says they gave heed to the things spoken by Philip when they heard and saw the signs which he did. So I know then what a sign is and it's purpose.

There are those who tell us that we don't believe God is doing anything because we don't believe God is performing miracles. Their concept is that if He is not performing miracles He's not doing anything. Of course, that's a total misunderstanding and people who have read their bible know that it is. The idea that some how or other God has to perform a miracle in order to do something is false. If a person reads his bible from the beginning of Genesis to the end of Revelations he will find out that there were a lot of things God did without performing a miracle. So that's a total misunderstanding. But, in the eyes of so many people today, their concept of a miracle is anything they don't understand. If they don't understand it, it's a miracle. I don't understand how a red cow can eat green grass and produce white milk but she does it but it's not a miracle. I certainly don't understand how a little computer chip can contain all the information that it does but it's not a miracle. So, just because I don't understand something doesn't mean it's a miracle.

HOW GOD ACTS

A miracle is that which transcends the natural . Some will say "that which is contrary to", no that's not so, it transcends it, it's over and above it. I think we can look at the New Testament and make it clear as to what we are talking about. In Lk. 22:50-51 the record says: **"And a certain one of them smote the servant of the high priest, and struck off his right ear. But Jesus answered and said, Suffer ye {them} thus far. And he touched his ear, and healed him."**

Chart #34
HOW GOD ACTS "Super Natural Source"
THROUGH MIRACLES Working above the plane of NATURAL law. (Transcends NATURAL law) **In Miracles He acts DIRECTLY.** Illustration: Mat. 8:26. Still a Storm. **THROUGH PROVIDENCE.** Utilizing NATURAL LAW. **In Providence He acts INDIRECTLY employing natural means.** Illustration: I Ki. 18:44,45

Now today if your ear is cutoff by accident, they can rush you into the hospital and they can re-attach that ear and through the process of healing that ear can be restored but that isn't what happened here. This transcended natural law. We are talking about natural law in our example and it required a time for healing but this happened immediately; that which transcended the natural law; it did not require a healing process. People will have an illness and when they go to the doctor and take the prescribed medicine and are healed, some will say "that was a miracle" but that's not what the bible describes as being a miracle. So, I submit to you that it is that which transcends the natural.

Turn with me to Jno. 20. In every debate I have had with the Charismatic preachers I have asked them the question: " Can the written record of miracles convince one to believe that Jesus is the Son of God? Can the written record do that?" You see their idea is that the written record is not sufficient, there must be more; there has to be the performance of miracles even today, but they are wrong. In Jno. 20:30-31, the record says: **"Many other signs therefore did Jesus in the presence of the disciples, which are not written in this book: but these are written, that ye may believe that Jesus is the Christ, the Son of God; and that believing ye may have life in his name."** What is so interesting about this is that in the text just prior to this Jesus just absolutely indicts those who demand that there be miracles today. Look at what he says in verse 26: **"And after eight days again his disciples were within, and Thomas with them. Jesus cometh, the doors being shut, and stood in the midst, and said, Peace {be} unto you. Then saith he to Thomas, Reach hither thy finger, and see my hands; and reach {hither} thy hand, and put it into my side: and be not faithless, but believing. Thomas answered and said unto him, My Lord and my God. Jesus saith unto him, Because thou hast seen me, thou hast believed: blessed {are} they that have not seen, and {yet} have believed.** The written record of miracles that are described to you and me today in the New Testament had not been completed. We did not see that happen but we believe it because of the written record of the miracles. So this idea that miracles have to be repeated for people to believe are indicted by Jesus as unbelievers. But there are those that will say to you and to me "If God is not performing miracles He's not doing anything" and of course that's not true. In their estimation it's an either or proposition; He's either performing miracles or He's not doing anything. Fact of the matter is, I've had brethren to say, in essence, the same thing to me.

Chart #35
EITHER OR PROPOSITION
IS IT ? Deism: Hands off policy – Does Nothing **OR** Charismatic: Must perform miracles to do anything Alternative: God providentially operates by natural law. Special Providence to the people of God. 1Pet. 3:10

The reason I decided to add this to my lessons is because in class, on this matter of indwelling, the statement was made that if the Holy Spirit doesn't actually indwell the child of God, then God can't do anything for him. You know, it surprised me because that's the same way the Charismatic will argue? So, their idea is that it is an either or proposition. What this amounts to is deism and they are accusing you and me of being Deist. That means that God set this universe into motion and then backed up to a shade tree and is watching to see what will happen, not doing anything. Just a hands off policy. I don't believe that and you don't believe that. The other extreme is that of the Charismatic who believes that He must perform a miracle to do anything. But you and I know that's not true either. The alternative between these two extremes is that God operates providentially through natural law as He has done since the beginning of our record from Genesis on down through the ages. The word "providence" only occurs one time in the bible, Acts 24:2, and it basically has to do with recognizing the need beforehand and making provisions for it. That's why Paul said, talking about the speaker," we appreciate your providence". There is a special providence for the people of God. Peter said ,(I Pet. 3:10): " **He that would love life and see good days, let him refrain his tongue from evil and his lips that they speak no guile let him say peace and pursue it for the eyes of the Lord are upon the righteous and His ears are open to their supplication.**" That's a special providence to the people of God.

Chart #36	
-- HOW GOD ACTS -- "Miracles & Providence"	
MIRACLE: Supernatural Means	**PROVIDENCE: Natural Means**
Virgin Birth (Mat. 1:18-25)	Samuel's Birth (I Sam. 1:6-20)
Miraculous Conception	Natural Means - Procreation
NOTE: GOD PERFORMED BOTH BOTH HAD A SUPERNATURAL SOURCE!	

Just exactly how does God act through providence? Anytime God acts you have something that is supernatural. In miracles that's the case; in providence that's the case. The point is that if God does something you have a supernatural source. But the particular means that are used does not have to be miraculous means. I don't know if you are following my reasoning or not. In other words, if God does it (anything at all) then that is a supernatural source. But that supernatural source does not have to use supernatural means, He can use natural law and that's what his providence is all about; using natural law to provide for the needs of His people.

Let me show you what I mean. On this side of the chart we have the case in I Sam. 1:6-20; where you have a discussion about Hannah, Elkanah her husband and Eli the priest. Hannah was barren and was sorely disturbed about this and was praying while standing in the temple. When Eli the priest saw that her lips were moving , he thought she was intoxicated. But she was pleading with the Lord that she might have a son. When this was made known, Eli said to her that God had heard her prayer and would answer it. Then the record says Elkanah knew his wife and she conceived and brought forth a son, Samuel. Did God do that? Yes He did but He did it by the natural means of procreation. The record says that God did it. God is the one that opened her womb that she might conceive yet it was by the natural process of procreation that brought about the birth of Samuel.

On the other side of the chart we have a supernatural source because God did it but you also have supernatural means in the birth of Jesus, (Mat. 1:18-25). An angel of the Lord spoke unto Joseph and told him not to reject Mary for her conception was a Holy thing. Luke's account, specifically, makes it clear that it was a miraculous conception. Did God do that? Well the bible says so. And so, you have both supernatural source and supernatural means in accomplishing it. So there is a difference in miracles and providence and the births of Samuel and Jesus illustrate that difference.

Providence is illustrated in Gen, 45:3-8. When Joseph's brothers sold him into captivity, it was because they hated him, they were jealous of him. Several years later when a famine was over all the earth, Joseph's brothers were effected by this drought. Joseph was down in Egypt where he was made governor over all the affairs of Egypt. Through his inspiration (a dream to which God gave him the interpretation and told him what needed to be done in order to preserve them through the famine years) the Egyptians had accumulated a large supply of food and it was necessary for his brothers to come there for food. They finally recognized Joseph and were frightened but Joseph said **"you didn't do this, God did it"**. Look at this, God was responsible, He had told Abraham that an evil nation would afflict his people for some 400 years. That was the land of Egypt. In getting the children of Israel into Egypt, the only time God touched the chain of events was in the interpretation of the dreams. Did God do it? Of course He did, he did it through natural means. All of the events that transpired: the coat of many colors; the jealousy of his brothers; in Potiphar's house where Potiphar's wife pursued Joseph, none of these events were miraculous. Read about all of these things that transpired and you will see that the only time God touched the events was in the interpretation of the dreams. He used natural means, His providence, His will to perform. The idea that He can't do anything without performing a miracle is just not so.

Chart #37
PROVIDENCIAL PRINCIPLES
1) GOD NEVER PROVIDENTIALLY ACTS CONTRARY TO HIS OWN REVEALED WILL 2) GOD NEVER PROVIDENTIALLY ACTS SO AS TO NEGATE MAN'S FREEDOM OF WILL 3) WE MUST DISTINGUISH BETWEEN **PROVIDENCE** & THE **MIRACULOUS** **NOTE:** In Providence God Utilizes His Natural Law - - **Indirectly** In the Miraculous God Acts in A Plane Above Natural Law - - **Directly** In Providence God works Behind the Scenes In the Miraculous He Acts Openly - - **Acts 3-4** • The Lame Man was Healed Miraculously • Adversaries Could Not Deny It **(4:14-16)**
UNDERSTANDING PROVIDENCE

There are some fundamental principles, when we talk about providence, that need to be respected .First of all, God never acts, providentially, contrary to His own nature or His revealed will. Secondly, He never acts, providentially, so as to negate man's freedom of will. He doesn't do that. Thirdly, we must distinguish between providence and the miraculous.

Now watch it, in providence God utilizes natural law and he does it indirectly. I believe with all my heart that God works through providence because the bible indicates that He does. But for me to point to some circumstance in my lifetime and say that was an act of God's providence , I don't have the right to do that and neither does anyone else. We had some preachers in Texas who thought they had this all worked out and low and behold they would point toward some instance where they had prayed for some brother who had become well and say "that was God's providence". When some of the brethren began to tell them they were preaching Pentecostalism, they squealed like a stuck pig, but that's what they were doing. You can not point toward something and say that was an act of God's providence. Even the inspired apostles would not do that. Onesimus was a slave who had left his master, Philemon, and had come into the presence of Paul. While in his presence Paul taught him the gospel and converted him. Began reading with me in verse 11. He said: **"who once was unprofitable to thee, but now is profitable to thee and to me: whom I have sent back to thee in his own person, that is, my very heart: whom I would fain have kept with me, that in thy behalf he might minister unto me in the bonds of the gospel: but without thy mind I would do nothing; that thy goodness should not be as of necessity, but of free will."** He is saying that I want to keep him but I want you to agree to it. Now read on where he says: **"For perhaps he was therefore parted {from thee} for a season, that thou shouldest have him for ever;"**

Chart #38		
MARK 16:17-20 **"Why Just Healing & Tongues?"**		
WHY **JUST**	**>>>**	**HEALING** **&** **TONGUES**
AND **NOT**	**>>>**	**DRINK DEADLY POISONS? OR TAKE UP SERPENTS?**
!????????????????????????????????!		

Even Paul would not say that God had a hand in this. He said perhaps which indicates that he was not certain. If Paul wouldn't say it then what right have I to decide that a specific act is God's providence. Who knows but by the providence of God I stand here before you now. But I don't know that. He works through providence but to be able to point toward something and say this is God's providence is a prerogative you don't have, you just don't have that ability. He works through natural law and He works <u>indirectly</u>. In miracles He works in a plane above natural law and He works directly. In providence God works behind the scenes and that's the reason why you don't know it. In miracles He works openly . In the 3rd and 4th chapters of the book of Acts where we read of the healing of the lame man, he was healed miraculously and the adversaries could not deny it. There is a difference in the two and I need to understand that God certainly works today; He works through providence. This is an area that needs to be addressed. With that in mind let's look now at Mk. 16:17-20. Jesus said in verses 17 and 18: **"And these signs shall accompany them that believe: in my name shall they cast out demons; they shall speak with new tongues;they shall take up serpents, and if they drink any deadly thing, it shall in no wise hurt them; they shall lay hands on the sick, and they shall recover."** I have pressed this point with the Pentecostal people and ask, "Why is it you just talk about healing and tongues?". They cite this passage and all they want to talk about and all they want to claim is healing and tongues. Why do they not pay attention to the matter of drinking deadly poison or taking up serpents? There have been those that have tried it. I, at one time had photographs of a lady who was bitten by a poisonous snake. I had a photograph of her three days later lying in her coffin. (I loaned those to somebody and never got them back and I don't remember who it was that I loaned them to.) So they have taken up poisonous snakes and they died after being bitten by them. But you know, they will tell us when we ask: "Now wait a minute preacher, if we did that we would be tempting God because that says if-,if-,if we drink any deadly thing. Now if we just accidentally do it we would not be harmed but we are not going to do it purposely because that would be tempting God". Well, they say it's all right for them to lay hands on the sick but look here it says "they shall take up serpents". So that doesn't say "if" does it? So they just leave poison out of the proposition because they know it will kill them. You see what I'm saying? They want to make a play on that word "if". They just look at the word "if" and say I can't do that but if it accidentally happened; but I can't deliberately do that. Now they will not apply that to the rest of the statement. It says they "shall" take up serpents and they "shall" lay hands on the sick . If "they shall lay hands on the sick" means they can deliberately do so then why not "they shall pick up serpents"? That's just a matter of trying to get around a difficulty because they don't want to pick up those snakes and they don't want to drink that deadly poison. They know it will kill them, there is not any doubt about it. So, I submit to you then that this question needs to be asked: "Why is it just healing and tongues that you want to observe"? That's the point they want to emphasize, healing and tongues.

I know , because the bible tells me, that these miracles were for a purpose. They were for the purpose of confirming the word of the person that spoke it; The matter of validating the man and validating the message.

I think this is a valid question and they need to address it. There are those that claim these signs and wonders and they are as woefully divided as the North is from the South. The Assemblies of God, for instance, teach that there are three persons in the Godhead and they claim signs and wonders. But the United Pentecostals say there is only one person in the Godhead and they also claim signs and wonders. Now then, is God confirming the message of these Assemblies of God preachers and also the message of these United Pentecostal preachers? If you ask them about it they won't answer. If you ask "are these people deceived?" They won't answer that. If you ask the other group if these over here are deceived, they won't answer that either. You know why, it's because both of them offer the same proofs for their practice and those proofs are the matter of the testimony of people. So, these people are widely divided and yet claim to be able to perform signs and wonders. The assemblies of God teach that water baptism is not essential and the United Pentecostals claim that it is. Here are two concepts that are diametrically opposed and we are asked to believe that God is confirming the teaching of both of these groups. He is not the author of confusion, (I Cor. 14:33). So I submit to you then, that they need to address these things and they will not do so. The bible teaches us that we not only have the right but also the obligation to test those who make such claims. John says **"Beloved, believe not every spirit but try the spirit because many false prophets are come out into the world."** So, we have the right, yea, we have the obligation to test them and that's exactly what we ought to do.

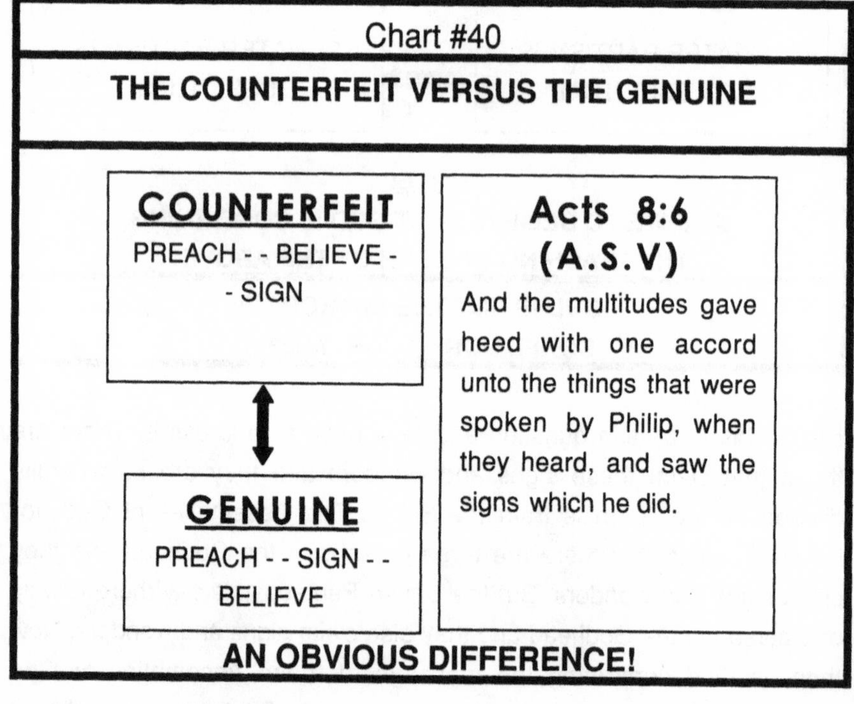

Here is a notable example of the counterfeit verse the genuine. In Acts8, Philip went down to Samaria and begin to preach the word. Now we know that Philip had the ability to perform signs and wonders because he did. And the record says: **"And the multitudes gave heed with one accord unto the things that were spoken by Philip, when they heard, and saw the signs which he did."** Note that the order of the genuine miracle is: Philip preached; he performed signs; that validated his message; and the people believed it. Now look at the counterfeit. These fellows will preach and say "if you believe we will perform a sign". That's a notable difference, isn't it? Someone may say "you don't think those fellows ever help the ones that they claim to heal?" Of course they do, but they do it at the expense of truth. You know as well as I that there are those who can think themselves into being sick. That's the kind of person that you can think them out of it. I tell you what, they cannot think them out of it if they don't believe in it; that's the power of suggestion and that's why they require faith on the part of the individual. When Amy Simple McPherson, in California, started her Four Square Gospel Group she was telling all of her people that it was wrong to go to a doctor, you will get into trouble she told them. She was out of circulation for about three weeks and when they found her she was in the hospital. She had a nervous break down and had to go to the hospital. At the same time she was claiming miracles, a French infidel was doing the same thing she was doing. You can do it, you can do it; it's the power of suggestion. There was a News Reporter way back then that reported these events, (and again I had that article and loaned it out and never got it back). It's interesting to note that these fellows will tell you that you have to believe or I can't do you any good and that's right, they cannot overcome unbelief as the apostles were able to do.

You will not sit here and let me tell you of how many of their services I have been in and have looked into and examined their claims and noted just how far off base they are. They do demand this, they say, "you have to believe or we cannot perform a sign". I tell you what, you will find 34 cases of healing in the New Testament and the best you can come up with is six on the account of personal faith. The rest of them have no faith indicated or involved the faith of someone else. Faith was not always necessary back then but it is for those today in order to perform "signs?".

What's the difference? One is counterfeit and one is genuine. They use the power of suggestion. That's exactly what they do.

THE GIFT OF THE SPIRIT

I talked to you earlier in the meeting about First Corinthians Chapters 12,13 and 14 and I only briefly mention this for the sake of time. In these chapters of First Corinthians you have Paul discussing the matter of the miraculous gifts of the Spirit. In the 12th Chapter they are named and in the 13th Chapter he tells how long they will last. We will take a look at that. In the 14th Chapter he gives the regulations that govern them. In I Cor. 12 the gifts are identified, there are nine of them listed and I want to take a little time to discuss these passages, and I think this is important for us to note. The gifts fall into three categories. There were those that dealt with intellectual powers. For instance : 1) Wisdom – The inside of the true nature of things according to W. E. Vine. 2) Knowledge- The ability to know, store and recall spiritual truth. 3) Faith – Special faith involved in the working of special miracles. All of these had to do with certain intellectual powers.

Chart #41

THE GIFT OF THE SPIRIT

INTELLECTUAL POWER

1) WISDOM: Insight into true nature of things (W.E. Vine)
2) KNOWLEDGE: Ability to know, store & recall spiritual truths
3) FAITH: Special faith involved in the working of miracles

EXHIBITION OF "MIRACULOUS FAITH"

1) Healing
2) Miracles (General)
3) Prophecy: Making known the mind of God
4) Discerning of Spirits: Detecting the false prophet

MIRACULOUS USE OF LANGUAGE

1) TONGUES: Miraculous Ability to Speak a Language
2) INTERPRETATION OF TONGUES: Miraculou Ability To Translate from One Language to Another

9 GIFTS: SUBDIVIDED INTO 3 GROUPS (1 Cor.12:8-10)

Then there were the exhibition of miraculous faith involved in: 1) Healing, 2) Miracles in general, 3) Prophecy, -- making known the mind of God, 4) Discerning of the spirits- detecting false prophets. You see, there were those in that day and age who could detect false prophets. How do we do it today? By this book, they didn't have the New Testament then so they needed special guidance, the discerning of spirits. Then you have : 1) Miraculous use of language -- the miraculous ability to speak a language in which they had not been tutored. 2) Interpretation of tongues – Miraculous ability to translate from one language to another. So, you have these nine gifts of the spirit divided up into three groups in I Cor. 12. These were the gifts and they were necessary because the written volume was not there for them to search out the truth as we are able to do today. I talked to you earlier of how these gifts were given. If there is any question in your mind, I invite you to read Acts 8:14-18. When Philip went down to Samaria he could not impart these gives but when the apostles arrived they did. The record says: **"Now when the apostles that were at Jerusalem heard that Samaria had received the word of God, they sent unto them Peter and John: who, when they were come down, prayed for them, that they might receive the Holy Spirit: for as yet it was fallen upon none of them: only they had been baptized into the name of the Lord Jesus.Then laid they their hands on them, and they received the Holy Spirit. Now when Simon saw that through the laying on of the apostles' hands the Holy Spirit was given..."** A simple illustration of this is that of a Sheriff. You elect a man to be Sheriff of this county and he has the authority to make an arrest. He has deputies and they can make an arrest but there are some things the Sheriff can do that the Deputies cannot do. That's true of the apostles and the prophets. The prophets could reveal divine truth but they could not impart this gift. Only the apostles, the ambassadors of the Lord, could do it. Thus, the apostles imparted those gifts. Its interesting to note in Romans Chapter One , Paul said to the church at Rome who had some gifts, (1:2): **"I desire to come to you that I might impart unto you some spiritual gift that you might be strengthened.** " They needed some they did not have. So, only the apostles were able to impart these gifts.

Chart #42
THE TONGUES OF THE NEW TESTAMENT
<u>TONGUES AS LANGUAGE</u> 1) Acts 2:6-9 - - SPEAK IN **<u>LANGUAGE</u>** 2) I Cor.. 14:9 - - WORDS **<u>UNDERSTOOD</u>** 3) Acts 19:6 - - SPOKE IN TONGUES & PROPHESIED 4) Acts 10:46 - - MAGNIFIED GOD **<u>TONGUES AS A SIGN TO UNBELIEVERS</u>** 1) 1 Cor. 14:22 - - SIGN TO UNBELIEVERS 2) Acts 2:5-12 - - UNBELIEVERS PRESENT 3) Acts 10:45 - - JEWS WITH PETER 4) Acts 19:1-6 - - SAME AS AT CORINTH (Received the Same Way By Paul) **NOTE: if not understandable Language - - not to be uttered (1Cor. 14:9, 27-28)**
UNDERSTANDABLE LANGUAGE

With that in mind then, turn with me to Acts 2. In this second chapter of Acts, when the Holy Spirit came on the day of Pentecost, there were some things that transpired that I want to take a look at. There was a sound of such great magnitude, like thunder, that the people around Jerusalem heard it. The record says when the sound was heard, and I'm reading in verse 2: **"And suddenly there came from heaven a sound as of the rushing of a mighty wind, and it filled all the house where they were sitting. And there appeared unto them tongues parting asunder, like as of fire; and it sat upon each one of them."** Visible tongues. You know that passage doesn't say there was any fire, there wasn't a spark of fire in this, this was simulated. The tongues were like as fire. Just as flames of fire will extend upward, so these were visible tongues that set upon the head of the apostles. You hear people say "come and see the Pentecost happen all over again". If it did, they would tare the building down getting out. They would for a fact if it actually happened because that sound and these visible tongues that set upon their heads would be enough to scare them out of their wits. They see the word fire and then assume that it is talking about baptism in fire and it doesn't say there was even a spark, it says like as fire. That just indicates they don't know what a figure of speech is, they don't know what a simile is. It was similar to this. The record continues to say, (verses 4-6): **"And they were all filled with the Holy Spirit, and began to speak with other tongues, as the Spirit gave them utterance. Now there were dwelling at Jerusalem Jews, devout men, from every nation under heaven. And when this sound was heard,"** The King James says when it was noised abroad. They will take this and say "well people went out and talked this thing up". That's not what that passage says, it was an inanimate sound like that of thunder. When this sound was heard, **"the multitude came together, and were confounded, "** [Why?] **"because that every man heard them speaking in his own language."** They spoke a language that they had not been tutored in. Those that heard pointed out that these men were all Galilaens and consequently did not know the language of all the nations present. There were about 16 or 17 nations present and nine different dialects. The apostles were able to address these people in their own tongues, their own dialect. Incidentally, you don't think for a moment that the miracle was in the ears of the hearers do you? There are those who think that. In as much as Peter's sermon was the one recorded, they think Peter preached it and everybody heard in their own language. No, that's not at all what that passage says. The miracle wasn't in the ear of the hearer, the miracle was in the tongue of the apostles. All of the apostles preached on the day of Pentecost, not just Peter. The eleven stood up and spoke. All the apostles were preaching. There were only nine different dialects, so there was no problem there. So they were preaching in every man's own language, language they had not been tutored in. Those who claim to be speaking in tongues today, if they go to a foreign country will have to learn that language. The apostles didn't have to do that. That's why Christ said to them **"you will be my witness in Jerusalem, in Judah and the uttermost parts of the earth"**, they could speak any language they had need of.

TONGUES IMPLY LANGUAGES

Look, if you will, at what the book has to say about tongues. It was a language, (Acts 2:6-8). In I Cor. 14:9, Paul said: **"So also ye, unless ye utter by the tongue speech easy to understood, how shall it be**

known what is spoken? for ye will be speaking into the air." So it was something that could be understood. He was talking about tongues. The record says, in Acts 19:6, "They spoke in tongues and prophesied". Paul, in I Cor.14:10-14, says prophesying was for teaching and edifying people and Acts 10:46 says it's for magnifying God. It's not a bunch of noise but words that can be understood and magnified God. Tongues are a sign to the unbelievers. I have been in their building and I urged them to speak in tongues and they said "We can't speak in tongues because there are unbelievers present". That was one of the purposes of it. Paul said tongues were signs to the unbelievers and when unbeliever were present, in Acts 2, they served as a sign to them. You know what, these people are taught that language they speak; these people who speak in tongues today. I learned it just as exactly and just as well as they did and would repeat it on my radio broadcast. They learned this and then get up and try to convince people that the Holy Spirit guided them. It was a bunch of gibberish, not an understandable language. In the bible it was an understandable language. So, the record said there were unbelievers present and the speaking in tongues was a sign to them. There were unbelievers present in Acts 2:5-12; there were unbelievers present in Acts 10, you remember we talked about Cornelius and when Peter went down and took those six Jews with him, there were unbelievers there, tongues magnified God, (Acts 10:45). The same at Corinth because it was received the same way by Paul,(Acts 19:1-6). So, I submit to you that tongues were signs to unbelievers. If it is not understandable language it's not to be uttered. You don't do it. I was sitting in the studio one time, waiting for my turn to present my radio broadcast and there was this woman preaching. She called herself the Queen of the South and I could tell you when she was about to utter this gibberish. It was whenever she lost her place in the manuscript she was reading.. I was sitting there watching her and ever time she lost her place she would utter this "tongue" and when she found her place the tongue speaking would be over.

FIRST CORINTHIANS 14

I want to go with you now to First Corinthians 14 and look at these tongues a little further. I have the text on the over head screen for your convenience. One of the things I want to emphasize is the word "unknown " Incidentally, this is published material and they are not as careful as they ought to be because those who print bibles and have some care and concern will italicize that word because it is not in the original Greek. There are those who find the word "unknown" italicized and they think it's there for emphasis but it's not. It's there to indicate that it has been supplied by the translators. All reputable printers will show that word in italics to indicate that it has been supplied by the translators. Anytime you see an italicized word it has been added, it wasn't in the original Greek Manuscript but the translators felt it needed to be there. What I want you to see is that every time the word "unknown" occurs in I Cor. 14, Paul is telling them don't do it! Don't do it! These Charismatics say "we speak in unknown tongues" but if so, they shouldn't because Paul said not to. He said that in verse 2: **"For he that speaketh in an unknown tongue speaketh not unto men, but unto God: for no man understandeth him".**

Chart #43
FIRST CORINTHIANS 14, (Part 1 of 3)
1 Follow after charity, and desire spiritual gifts, but rather that ye may prophesy. **2** For he that speaketh in an unknown tongue speaketh not unto men, but unto God: for no man understandeth him; howbeit in the spirit he speaketh mysteries. **3** But he that prophesieth speaketh unto men to edification, and exhortation, and comfort. **4** He that speaketh in an unknown tongue edifieth himself; but he that prophesieth edifieth the church. **5** I would that ye all spake with tongues but rather that ye prophesied: for greater is he that prophesieth than he that speaketh with tongues, except he interpret, that the church may receive edifying. **6** Now, brethren, if I come unto you speaking with tongues, what shall I profit you, except I shall speak to you either by revelation, or by knowledge, or by prophesying, or by doctrine? **7** And even things without life giving sound, whether pipe or harp, except they give a distinction in the sounds, how shall it be known what is piped or harped? **8** For if the trumpet give an uncertain sound, who shall prepare himself to the battle? **9** So likewise ye, except ye utter by the tongue words easy to be understood, how shall it be known what is spoken? for ye shall speak into the air.

Then look at what he said in verse 9: **"So likewise ye, except ye utter by the tongue words easy to be understood, how shall it be known what is spoken? for ye shall speak into the air.** " So, he says if you do that nothing comes of it but a lot of hot air and they think it means do it when every one of these passages says don't do it. Look here , **"He that speaks in an unknown tongue edifieth himself but he that prophecy edifies the church."** In other words, he may speak in that unknown language but nobody else is edified as a result of it. The thrust of I Cor. 14 was this matter that they were making a display out of speaking in tongues. They could speak in tongues but the audience could not understand it and that's why they were not suppose to do it.

For the sake of time, drop down to verse 6 where he says: **"Now, brethren, if I come unto you speaking with tongues, what shall I profit you, except I shall speak to you either by revelation, or by knowledge, or by prophesying, or by doctrine? And even things without life giving sound, whether pipe or harp, except they give a distinction in the sounds, how shall it be known what is piped or harped?"** If the troops are in the field, for instance, and when the trumpeter sounds the trumpet in battle, if he sounds the wrong notes they wouldn't know whether to retreat or advance. So, he said whatever it is that serves as a means of communication must give a distinct sound. That's the purpose of words an thus, that is why he says in verse 9: **"So likewise ye, except ye utter by the tongue words easy to be understood, how shall it be known what is spoken? for ye shall speak into the air."** It's interesting to note that in verse 10, these two words "voices" and "signification", mean the same thing in the Greek:**"There are, it may be, so many kinds of voices in the world, and none of them is without <u>signification</u>."**

So he is saying there are many different kinds of voices but a voice is not a voice unless it signifies something. It has to make something known and this gibberish that the Charismatic use doesn't really mean anything, it's not a language it's just noise. In verse 13 he says: **"Wherefore let him that speaketh in an <u>unknown</u> tongue pray that he may interpret. For if I pray in an <u>unknown</u> tongue, my spirit prayeth, but my understanding is unfruitful."**

Chart #44

FIRST CORINTHIANS 14, (Part 2 of 3)

10 There are, it may be, so many kinds of voices in the world, and
none of them is without signification.**11** Therefore if I know not the
meaning of the voice, I shall be unto him that speaketh a barbarian,
and he that speaketh shall be a barbarian unto me. **12** Even so ye,
forasmuch as ye are zealous of spiritual gifts, seek that ye may excel
to the edifying of the church. **13** Wherefore let him that speaketh in an
unknown tongue pray that he may interpret. **14** For if I pray in an
unknown tongue, my spirit prayeth, but my understanding is unfruitful.
15 What is it then? I will pray with the spirit, and I will pray with the
understanding also: I will sing with the spirit, and I will sing with the
understanding also.**16** Else when thou shalt bless with the spirit, how
shall he that occupieth the room of the unlearned say Amen at thy
giving of thanks, seeing he understandeth not what thou sayest? **17**
For thou verily givest thanks well, but the other is not edified. **18** I
thank my God, I speak with tongues more than ye all: **19** Yet in the
church I had rather speak five words with my understanding, that by
my voice I might teach others also, than ten thousand words in an
unknown tongue.

There is some misunderstanding about what the word "understanding" means in this text but let's read on: **"What is it then? I will pray with the spirit, and I will pray with the understanding also: I will sing with the spirit, and I will sing with the understanding also."** So I submit to you that "understanding" is named when " being understood" is intended.

The New American Standard on this particular passage, plays right into the hands of the Charismatic and they misinterpret it's meaning. So, the term "understand" is named when "being understood" is intended. It is not unusual for a figure of speech to be used that way. How do I know that? I am going to show you why I know it. He says: **"Else when thou shalt bless with the spirit, how shall he that occupieth the room of the unlearned"** [that's one who doesn't understand the language] **"say Amen at thy giving of thanks, seeing he understandeth not what thou sayest? "** The whole point of I Cor. 14 is to be understood; I'll sing with the spirit, I'll sing so as to be understood. This is why, brethren, I have problems with some of the group singing. You get it on a tape and you try to understand what the words are. Singing is suppose to teach and admonish. But you listen to some of the groups singing and you can't understand the words. I heard a radio broadcast and the fellow talked about 10 minutes preaching about vocal music and against instrumental music and bless his heart he put on three tapes of Acappella music and you couldn't understand a word that was said. It sounded good but you couldn't understand it. Yet, I must sing to be understood. Why is that true? It's because we are to teach and admonish by our singing. Paul said; I'll sing with spirit; I'll pray with the spirit; I'll sing with the understanding; I'll pray with the understanding. If I don't do that, the one who occupies the seat of the unlearned will not understand what I am saying.

Chart #45
FIRST CORINTHIANS 14, (Part 3 of 3)
20 Brethren, be not children in understanding: howbeit in malice be ye children, but in under-standing be men. **21** In the law it is written, With men of other tongues and other lips will I speak unto this people; and yet for all that will they not hear me, saith the Lord. **22** Wherefore tongues are for a sign, not to them that believe, but to them that believe not: but prophesying serveth not for them that believe not, but for them which believe. **23** If therefore the whole church be come together into one place, and all speak with tongues, and there come in those that are unlearned, or unbelievers, will they not say that ye are mad? **24** But if all prophesy, and there come in one that believeth not, or one unlearned, he is convinced of all, he is judged of all: **25** And thus are the secrets of his heart made manifest; and so falling down on his face he will worship God, and report that God is in you of a truth. **26** How is it then, brethren? when ye come together, every one of you hath a psalm, hath a doctrine, hath a tongue, hath a revelation, hath an interpretation. Let all things be done unto edifying. **27** If any man speak in an unknown tongue, let it be by two, or at the most by three, and that by course; and let one interpret. **28** But if there be no interpreter, let him keep silence in the church; and let him speak to himself, and to God.

So, "understand" is named when "being understood" is intended. Thus, again the unknown tongue (language) is not to be spoken in our assemblies. These folks that claim to have miraculous gifts of the Spirit violate every principle in 1Cor. 14 that governs them. Let me show you, in verse 27 Paul writes: **"If any man speak in an unknown tongue, let it be by two, or at the most by three, and that by course; and let one interpret. But if there be no interpreter, let him keep silence in the church; and let him speak to himself, and to God."** That language means at least two and at the most three and he says when that happens, you let one of them interpret. Why? Because he is speaking a language that the audience does not know. Then he says if there is no interpreter, let him keep silence in the church. That means keep his mouth shut. Do the tongue speakers do that? No, they don't do that. They pay no attention to what Paul says about the matter. They will tell you: "Well this is just spontaneous, we can't help it." Oh yes they can, Look at what verse 32 says: **"And the spirits of the prophets are subject to the prophets."** They do not have to do it, the one that has the gift has control of that gift, the gift doesn't control them.

Chart #46
DURATION OF TONGUES
<u>**I Cor. 13:8-13**</u> "Love never faileth: but whether {there be} prophecies, they shall be done away; whether {there be} tongues, they shall cease; whether {there be} knowledge, it shall be done away. For we know in part, and we prophesy in part; but when that which is perfect is come, that which is in part shall be done away. When I was a child, I spake as a child, I felt as a child, I thought as a child: now that I am become a man, I have put away childish things. For now we see in a mirror, darkly; but then face to face: now I know in part; but then shall I know fully even as also I was fully known. But now abideth faith, hope, love, these three; and the greatest of these is love."

They 're wrong and everything they have to say about it is wrong. Paul said in this instance : **"let it be by two, or at the most by three, and that by course; and let one interpret. But if there be no interpreter, let him keep silence in the church"** So they violate that principle, they do not act in such a way as to edify each other. No one is edified, they may be emotionalized but they are not edified because they haven't understood anything. Paul writes in v26, "let all things be done unto edifying."

Now, look at the other principle . Paul says: **"For God is not the author of confusion, but of peace, as in all churches of the saints"** And what the Charismatics do is mass confusion! You listen to it; it's mass confusion. So, they violate that principle as well. They also violate the principle in verse 34. Where Paul says: **"Let your women keep silence in the churches: for it is not permitted unto them to speak; but they are commanded to be under obedience as also saith the law"** They violate that also. And they violate verse 40: **"Let all things be done decently and in order."** If you watch one of these Charismatic programs and if you have a split screen, (I can't afford one), just turn the second screen to a rock and roll program and turn the sound off and compare the two. Look at them; mass confusion and they do all of that in the name of religion. So, I submit to you that First Corinthians 14 condemns them in no uncertain terms.

Paul says , in I Cor. 13, starting in verse 1: **"Love never faileth: but whether {there be} prophecies, they shall be done away; whether {there be} tongues, they shall cease; whether {there be} knowledge, it shall be done away.** Incidentally, you'll note that Paul mentions prophecies, tongues, and knowledge, one out of each of the three categories that I mentioned to you before. Remember those three categories of gifts? Paul selected one out of each of those categories. This again is a figure of speech called synecdoche where a part of these gifts are named and the entirety of the gifts are intended. Paul took one out of each of those three categories. He said love never fails but where there be prophecies they shall be done away. Where there be tongues they shall cease and where there be knowledge it shall be done away. That was the miraculous knowledge given by the Spirit. Then he said in verse 9: **"For we know in part, and we prophesy in part but when that which is perfect is come, that which is in part shall be done away."** Here we have a contrast. Remember, I was talking to you last night about contrast? This word "part" is set in contrast to the word "perfect". What does "part" mean? Well it means partial, not all, that's what a part of something is. What is the opposite of partial,? It's complete. It's not that difficult. That's what the word perfect means, it means complete. Look at it now, prophesy in part (partial) but when that which is perfect (complete) comes that which is in part (partial) shall be done away. Look now at Paul's illustration: **"When I was a child, I spake as a child, I felt as a child, I thought as a child: now that I am become a man, I have put away childish things."** Watch this closely. He said; **"For now we see in a mirror, darkly;"** In other words, if you had a piece of polished steel, and that's what they used for a mirror back then, and you rubbed SOS pad across the face of it, you know what you would see. You couldn't see yourself very well and so he said I see in a mirror darkly: **"but then face to face: now I know in part; "** [when that which is perfect come] **"but then shall I know fully even as also I was fully known."** The illustration is about him looking in a mirror and seeing himself partially. But, when that which is perfect is come, by way of comparison, he will see himself fully or as he really is. Then he said now I know in part but then I will know fully. Paul lays it out precisely; know in part, know fully. That's what I was talking to you about up above. That which is fully is that which is perfect or complete. Thus, this had to do with partial revelation. We'll note that in the chart in just a moment. All the gospel wasn't revealed and recorded at the same time. They had earthen vessels, inspired men and thus, as for as the message of Christ was concerned, it was partial. That's what that passage indicates. Paul said now I know in part, then I shall know fully.

CONTRAST ILLUSTATION

This will illustrate those contrasts we have been talking about. You will note in this passage we've just read we have the contrast illustrated. You will note that each partakes of the nature of the other. Through the many years , I've not once got one of these fellow to look at this much less try to answer it. An illustration is trying to amplify and make clear the point that's being made.

The Contrasts Are:

1) When I was a child I spoke as a child but when I became a man I spoke as a man, in other words there is the infant stage and the manhood stage.
2) I see in a mirror darkly now but then face to face. Each one partaking of the nature of the other.

3) Now I know in part but then I shall know fully. The illustrations show that during the infant stage of the church, these signs and miracles were necessary. But they are not necessary today because we have the completely revealed will of Christ recorded in the New Testament.

Chart #47
CONTRAST ILLUSTRATION
In I Cor. 13 "A CHILD" v.11 "A MAN" "A MIRROR" v.12 "FACE TO FACE" "KNOW PART" v.13 "KNOW FULLY" **ILLUSTRATIONS APPLIED:** **"IN PART" versus "PERFECT":** Signs & Wonders The Completely REVEALING, **verses** REVEALED, CONFIRMING, **verses** CONFIRMED & RECORDING **verses** RECORDED WORD OF GOD or WILL OF GOD
EACH PARTAKES NATURE OF THE OTHER

The Illustration Applied.

1) In part applied: signs and wonders revealing and confirming the will of God, verses 9 and 10.
2) That which is perfect applied: the completely revealed and recorded will of God.

In light of the context of the passage and in the light of what the bible teaches about the purpose of these signs to confirm the word, that becomes evident. There are those who see this word "perfect" and they think it means sinless and since Christ was sinless it means when Christ comes again. But if you stop and think about that you realize they don't really believe that. If their concept of 1Corinthians 13 is right , they will argue that since people still know something now that which is perfect hasn't come yet. They take that word "knowledge" to mean knowing something. So, their idea leads to the conclusion that when Christ comes we won't know anything. Do you see what that does to heaven?

According to their argument on this :"We still have knowledge and that proves that which is perfect hasn't come. " "That which is perfect is the second coming of Christ. " **Conclusion:** When he comes we won't have any knowledge anymore, we will just be idiots in heaven, we won't know anything. The knowledge of I Cor. 12 and 13 was miraculous knowledge, not something you obtain from study. When all is said and done and if you look at it honestly, it doesn't take Solomon to see that we are looking at the confirmed will of the Lord.

A CONTRAST IN WALK

There was a period of time when all of the word was oral, it was in men. Paul said it was in earthen vessels. During this section under discussion (see the chart), all of it was oral, none of it was written. Just how long this was the case, I don't know. Then there was a period of time when part of it was oral and part of it was written. In II Thes. 2:15. Paul said: **"So then, brethren, stand fast, and hold the traditions which ye were taught, whether by word, or by epistle of ours."** Thus, in Eph. 3:4 Paul said: " **whereby, when ye read, ye can perceive my understanding in the mystery of Christ;"** This passage says when that which is perfect comes that which is in part shall be done away. What is that which is in part? That is the matter of partial revelation during the age of these miraculous gifts and he points out that when this happened (partial done away) that these (the written) would remain, (Heb. 2:1-4). So, the New Testament teaches concerning signs and miracles that they were necessary because the word was not written.

I was in a conversation with a young preacher one time and we were talking about signs and wonders and he said to me: "You make God a respecter of persons." I said: "Oh, how is that ?" He said: " they had signs and wonders back then and you say we don't have them now so that proves God is a respecter of persons". I handed him my New Testament and said: "Did Philip have that?" He said: "What do you mean?" I said: "you know what I mean. Did Philip have a written New Testament?" He said: "No." I said: "Was God a respecter of persons then?"

You know, if a person can understand that they can understand why it was necessary there be these signs and wonders during that age. We have this book, this message; this is what tells us how to be saved; this is what tells us how to worship; It tells us about the work and organization of the church, it will judge us in the time of judgment. (Jno. 12:47-48).

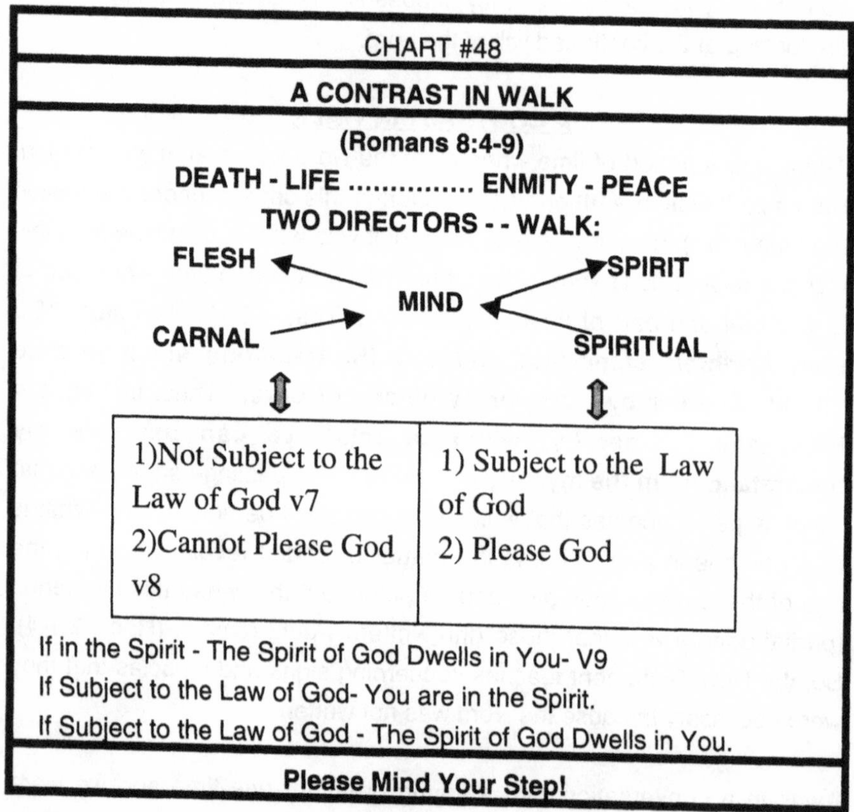

The End of Lesson Four

CHAPTER FIVE

"Holy Spirit Indwelling"

I am glad of this opportunity to discuss the subject of the indwelling of the Holy Spirit with you. There are a number of passages that are used in order to try to prove some direct effect of the Holy Spirit either directly dwelling in ones body or having some direct effect on their lives. What has been surprising to me, through the years, is that the same passages the Charismatic will use in an effort to prove direct miraculous effects in their lives are the very same passages that some of our brethren use to try to prove direct indwelling. Let me show you what I am talking about. One of the passages they use is Rom. 8:9: **"But you are not in the flesh but in the Spirit, if indeed the Spirit of God dwells in you. Now if anyone does not have the Spirit of Christ, he is not His."** The issue is not that the Spirit of God dwells in the Christian, the issue is how the Spirit dwells in him. That is what we will be discussing. Acts 2:38 is another one that is used and I will talk about it in just a little while.

JOHN 7:37-39:

Every discussion I have had about this subject, whether it be about the miraculous effect of the Holy Spirit or the direct indwelling of the Spirit, I am confronted with this passage in Jno. 7:37-39: **"On the last day, that great day of the feast, Jesus stood and cried out, saying, 'If anyone thirsts, let him come to Me and drink. He who believes in Me, as the Scripture has said, out of his heart will flow rivers of living water.' But this He spoke concerning the Spirit, whom those believing in Him would receive; for the Holy Spirit was not yet given, because Jesus was not yet glorified."** All they see in that text is the fact that the passage says, "which they that believe on Him would receive". I have had this passage used where someone would argue that this is talking about Holy Spirit Baptism and I have had some of my brethren declare that this is talking about the Holy Spirit indwelling the body. That is strange isn't it? I do not believe it is talking about either one of those things. It is talking about the mission that the Holy Spirit would accomplish when He came. We talked about that in our very first lesson.

Acts 5:32, that I also mentioned to you earlier, is another one of the passages that is used where it says: **"And we are His witnesses to**

these things, and so also is the Holy Spirit whom God has given to those who obey Him." This same passage is used by both of these groups that we are talking about. Then Gal. 4:6 says: **"And because you are sons, God has sent forth the Spirit of His Son into your hearts, crying out, "Abba, Father!"** These are the passages that are used to prove both Holy Spirit Baptism and indwelling of the Holy Spirit.

Chart #49
THE ISSUE:
NEGATIVE: (IT IS NOT) 1. DOES the Holy Spirit CONVICT MEN? 2. DOES the Holy Spirit LEAD MEN? 3. DOES the Holy Spirit INDWELL THE CHRISTIAN? **POSITIVE: (IT IS)** 1. How does He, CONVICT, LEAD & INDWELL MEN? 2. DOES He act DIRECTLY? … Or, does He act INDIRECTLY through MEDIUM
HOW DOES HE DO IT?

But these passages are not talking about what these fellows claim that they are, not at all. The only difference in the response about this is that our brethren will tell us that they don't really know what the Holy Spirit does for them. They just believe that He is in their body. However, some have attributed to the Holy Spirit the act of helping them find a better parking place or helping them find a better job. This is an area that needs a lot of investigation but I am not going to do it now. Certainly God works through His providence and we talked about that last night. If I didn't believe that God was doing something and helping people, I would not bother to pray. You believe that He does too. You pray for someone who is ill but you don't expect some miracle to be accomplished. We believe He works indirectly through some medium. So, I thought it would be interesting to reflect upon the fact that these are the same passages that all of these folks use. The issue needs to be clearly set out as we talk about these things. It is not "Does the Holy Spirit convict men of sin?" There are those who charge that "Well you don't believe the Holy Spirit convicts men of sin". Well I do and you do too. They are by this kind of like they are by Jno. 3:16, they don't know what the rest of that passage says, convicting of sin and righteousness to come, and Jesus goes on to explain that. All they see is the conviction of sin and I believe that He does convict men. I also believe He leads men. If He is not leading you, you are not a child of God, Rom. 8:14. And I believe He indwells the Christian because the bible says that He does. But, that is not the issue. The issue is: How does He convict, lead, and indwell men? He does all of these things in the same way and He also makes elders, Acts 20:28. He bears witness with our spirit that we are Sons of God. So, all of these things, I believe, He does in exactly the same way. Anything the record says the Holy Spirit does today, I believe He does it in precisely the same way.

THE QUESTION

How does He convict, lead and indwell men? Does He act directly or does He act indirectly through some medium? I have used this illustration several times and I think it is a pretty good one. I call attention to the fact that some one has been ill for some time and you see him some time later and he is really looking fine. You say, man you sure look good, what happened? He says well the doctor healed me. Well, did he do it directly or did he do it indirectly through some medium or medication? He did it indirectly. The doctor did it but he did it indirectly, through some medium. So, the question is: How does the Holy Spirit do these things? Does He do it directly, separate and apart from some medium or does He do it indirectly through some medium? How does He do what He does today?

Someone charges that you don't believe in the Holy Spirit because you don't believe as they do about how the Holy Spirit operates. The fellow who does not believe in the Holy Spirit is the fellow who does not believe what the Holy Spirit says about Himself and that is what we want to consider; what does the Holy Spirit say about Himself? So, I categorically charge that there are some that do not believe in the Holy Spirit because they do not believe what the Holy Spirit has to say. Those on the day of Pentecost were convicted of sin and the Holy Spirit convicted them but the record says in verse 37, "Now when they heard these things" and that is how they were convicted; it was by the message they heard: " **Now when they heard this, they were cut to the heart, and said to**

Peter and the rest of the apostles, 'Men and brethren, what shall we do?' Then Peter said to them, 'Repent, and let every one of you be baptized in the name of Jesus Christ for the remission of sins; and you shall receive the gift of the Holy Spirit'." Now what does that mean? In this first part of our lesson we will deal with the "Gift of the Holy Spirit". We will deal with the idea of indwelling in the latter part of the lesson. So I pose the question: Does that mean that the Holy Spirit is the gift or does it mean the Holy Spirit is the giver? You see, you do not settle that question by simply saying the Holy Spirit is the gift. Really! How do you know that the Holy Spirit is not the giver? Incidentally, this is the only time I know of where people will have the gift and the giver to be the same thing. Think about that for moment. They have the gift and the giver being the same. Any time there is a gift; there is a giver. If there is a gift, there has to be some object to receive it.

Chart #50
TO GIVE -OR- BE GIVEN
ACTS 2:38 **"GIFT OF THE HOLY SPIRIT"** **<u>QUESTION:</u>** **Is the Holy Spirit** **The Gift** **- or -** **The GIVER?** **<u>ILLUSTRATION:</u>** **Gift of the FORD FOUNDATION:** **The GIFT or the GIVER?**
That Is Our Question!

What they claim in this is that the Holy Spirit is both the gift and the giver. I tell you frankly, it does not answer the question to just say "the bible says receive the Holy Spirit and that means the Holy Spirit is the gift". No, it does not mean that for He may just as well be the giver in this grammatical structure. If I talk about receiving the gift of the Ford Foundation, I don't think anyone would think that I received the Ford

Foundation as the gift. They would understand that was a gift the Ford Foundation gave. The fact of the matter is, I know of no other circumstance where you have similar language and people reason as they do here. The only time people will take an expression such as that of the gift of the Holy Spirit and decide the gift is the Holy Spirit is in this passage of Acts 2:38. That is what is so disturbing to me, the inconsistency of their thinking. Let me show you what I am talking about. The particular grammar of the text will not settle the issue. Men have argued both ways. Some will say, "Well the grammar will prove that the Holy Spirit is the gift". Another will argue "Well that says the Holy Spirit is the giver". When all is said and done all of these sources they have examined states that in the final analysis you cannot determine the meaning on the basis of grammar but on the basis of theology. Brother Frank Pucket with this in a little booklet and he says, and I agree with him whole heartily, "I am not willing to let those sectarian scholars determine my theology for me." And that is what they all say. You can not settle it on grammar brethren; I guarantee that you cannot because I have heard it argued both ways. When all is said and done, these same authorities that they cite will tell you that it is not settled on the basis of grammar but on the basis of theology. I believe we can settle it by looking at it in the light of the book. I put the original Greek word for gift in these passages so that you would know that the same word is used in every one of these passages (*dorea, dorea, dorea*). In Jno. 4:10 when Jesus was talking to the woman at the well, He said if you had known who it was that you were talking to and if you had asked for the gift of God, He would have given you "Living Water". So, you have the "gift of God", the same structure as in Acts 2:38. In Eph. 4:7 when Paul was talking about those gifts of the Spirit; He said there was a distribution of the grace of God and that the "gift of Christ" was involved in that distribution of those gifts that they received. So, again you have the same structure. You have the "gift of God" and you have the "gift of Christ" and in Acts 2:38 you have the "gift of the Holy Spirit". These statements are always the same. Why is it, do you suppose, that brethren do not think that in the "gift of God' that God is the gift. They know that God is the giver in that case. And neither do they believe that Christ is the gift. Why then do they insist that the Holy Spirit is the gift in Acts 2:38? In these first two passages, Christ and God are the giver's. In each of these passages, you have the same word for gift (*dorea*); you have the same structure; they are all used in the same sense specifying what the Holy Spirit, God and Christ are doing.

Chart #51

THE GIFT (DOREA)

1. "The gift (Dorea) of God" - - Jno. 4:10

That which God would Give ... Living Water.

2. "The gift (Dorea) of Christ" - - Ephesians 4:7

That which Christ would give...grace in the distribution of spiritual gifts.

3 "The gift (Dorea) of the Holy Spirit" -Acts 2:38

That which the Holy Spirit would give... the salvation & blessing of the promise-2:21,30.

CONCLUSION: In each of the above passages you have the same word for gift. You have the same structure. They are all used in the same sense, specifying what God, Christ, & the Holy Spirit are doing.

QUESTION: What kind of logic will cause me to argue that in the first two God & Christ are the GIVERS but in the third the Holy Spirit is the GIFT?

THE OBVIOUS TRUTH

1. The Gift of God is not God -- But something God gives.
2. The Gift of Christ is not Christ -- But something Christ gives.
3. The Gift of the Holy Spirit is not the Holy Spirit -- But something the Holy Spirit gives

HOLY SPIRIT IS THE GIVER

THE QUESTION IS:

What kind of logic will cause me to argue that in the first two, God and Christ are the giver's but in the third, the Holy Spirit is the gift? I think consistency will demand they be interpreted the same way. What you can prove about the Holy Spirit you can also prove about the Father and the Son. So, the gift of God is not God Himself but that which God gives. The gift of Christ is not Christ but something Christ would give. Likewise, the gift of the Holy Spirit is not Himself but something that the Holy Spirit gives. So, the expression "gift of the Holy Spirit" in Acts 2:38 is not talking about the Holy Spirit but something the He would give. I know that the Holy Spirit is the giver of gifts, (I Cor. 12:8-9). So, I am on target there, the Holy Spirit is the giver of gifts. I want to talk to you about this in the immediate context. I know that I talked to you about what context is, at least what I am convinced about its importance. It involves the statement, it involves that which immediately precedes and follows it and it involves all other related facts. The first thing I want to do is to look at the immediate context. In Acts 2:33, the Apostle Peter said: **"Therefore being exalted to the right hand of God, and having received from the Father the promise of the Holy Spirit, He poured out this which you now see and hear."**

Chart #52
THE GIFT & THE PROMISE
A COMPARISON Acts 2:33 "Received the PROMISE of the Holy Spirit" **NOTE:** He did not receive the Holy Spirit... He received what the Holy Spirit PROMISED! - Acts 2:38 "Received the GIFT of the Holy Spirit" NOTE: They did not receive the Holy Spirit... They received what the Holy Spirit GAVE!
What He Promised & Gave?

So, you have the statement, "received the promise of the Holy Spirit". In verse 38, you have a parallel statement, "receive the gift of the Holy Spirit". Look at these two statements: received the promise; received the gift of the Holy Spirit. Just five verses apart and in the very same sermon preached by the Apostle Peter. Now, does this mean that Jesus received the Holy Spirit? Or, does it mean that He received what the Holy Spirit promised? Just think for a moment. You know that it would not make good "nonsense" to assume that when the Lord ascended back to the Father that He received the Holy Spirit. The Apostle Peter, in that same sermon, pointed out that what He received was what the Holy Spirit promised. What the Holy Spirit promised was that He would sit on David's throne. The Holy Spirit made that promise through David. For many years in the early part of this century there were many in the Church of our Lord who argued that the premillennial concept was right and that the Lord was going to come back and establish an earthly kingdom. One of the things they argued was that He intended to establish a kingdom when He came but because the Jews rejected Him, He established the church instead. Then, they argued, He is going to return and establish His kingdom He intended to establish the first time. First of all. our brethren pointed out that they were wrong about this because Paul writes, in Eph. 3:10-11, that the church is in the mind of God in eternity. Secondly, Our brethren pointed out that Peter said Jesus was on His throne in Acts 2. If He was on His throne, He obviously had a kingdom to rule over: **"Therefore being exalted to the right hand of God, and having received from the Father the promise of the Holy Spirit, He poured out this which you now see and hear."**

In Tampa Florida, a few years back, I was meeting a man named Tom Sharp on the subject of present day miracles and the Godhead. His concept of miracles and such was expressed by him when he said "Now if this was the kingdom age, I would agree with Mr. Moore because in the kingdom age these will not be needed". Well, you know what I did, I said you have given up your proposition because we are in the kingdom age. Do you know how I proved it? I went to this statement in Acts 2. I want to read it to show you that I am on target with this. This passage states that the Holy Spirit promised something and inspired David to write it. Thus, the Holy Spirit is named when what the Holy Spirit enabled David to write was intended. But beginning in Verse 32 Peter says: **"This Jesus God has raised up, of which we are all witnesses. Therefore being exalted to the right hand of God, and having received from the Father the promise of the Holy Spirit, He poured out this which you now see and hear. For David did not ascend into the heavens, but he says himself: 'The Lord said to my Lord, "Sit at My right hand, till I make Your enemies Your footstool.'** " He also made the same statement earlier in verse 30 when he said: **"Therefore, being a prophet, and knowing that God had sworn with an oath to him that**

of the fruit of his body, according to the flesh, He would raise up the Christ to sit on his throne," I said to Mr. Sharp, this passages says that Jesus is on the right hand of God exalted and what He received of the Father was what the Holy Spirit promised. What the Holy Spirit promised was that He would sit on the throne of David. Peter said He had received that and thus, He was on His throne at that very time. So I said to the audience "Mr. Sharp has given up his proposition. I pressed him on this. I believe he gave up because he did not try to answer me on this. We are in the kingdom age. I think he gave up the debate because that passage says that what Jesus received was what the Holy Spirit promised and what the Holy Spirit promised was that He would receive a kingdom and a throne. Now, if that means He received the promise, and it does, then why would anybody have difficulty in understanding that to "receive the gift of the Holy Spirit" is talking about the gift the Holy Spirit would give? What He promised, He gave. So, I submit to you that right in this same text you have comparable language showing that He received the promise of the Holy Spirit, He did not receive the Holy Spirit.

Chart #53
"GIFT" IMPLIES:
<u>Jno. 4:10</u>
1. GIVER .... GOD
2. RECEIVER .....ONE WHO ASKS
3. THE GIFT ...... LIVING WATER
<u>Acts 2:38</u>
1. GIVER .... HOLY SPIRIT
2. RECEIVER . .BAPTIZED PENITENT
3. THE GIFT . . . ANY & ALL BLESSINGS IN CHRIST
<u>EXAMPLE</u>
1. GIVER ....EMPLOYER
2. RECEIVER ....EMPLOYEE
3. THE GIFT, SALARY- INSURUANCE &ETC.
Consider All Implications!

The gift of the Holy Spirit is the gift that the Holy Spirit gives. I suggested to you earlier that a gift implies something. A gift implies a giver and it implies a receiver. So, in Jno. 4:10 the giver is God and Jesus said to that woman at the well "if you had asked He would of given you the gift of God". So, the receiver is the one who asks and the gift was the Living Water. The text show that. In Acts 2:38 the giver is the Holy Spirit, the receiver is the baptized penitent, the gift is any and all blessings in Christ.

EXAMPLE

In the work place the giver is the employer, the receiver is the employee and the gift is salary and all fringe benefits such as insurance, sick leave, retirement provision and etc. So, there are some implications in our text. When this passage talks about a gift it implies something and we must infer what is implied. It implies a giver, it implies someone who receives and it implies the gift. It makes no sense to me to make the giver and the gift one and the same thing. I believe it to be fallacious to reason after such a fashion. The Apostle Peter, who was speaking on that occasion, was explaining what was taking place. Some had charged that these men were drunk but Peter said, **"no they are not drunk seeing it is only the third hour of the day".** He said this is that which was spoken of by the Prophet Joel. Peter said that Joel prophesied that something would happen in the last days,(Joel 2). You understand that Peter was saying that the last days had begun. Last days simply means the last period of time that God would deal with people in relation to time. So, he said this is that which Joel prophesied, **"He would pour out His Spirit on all flesh".** I have stated in my younger days that this occasion in Acts 2 and the conversion of Cornelious in Acts 10 fulfilled this promise. I now know better because that is not what the passages is talking about. Obviously, the passage implies something that the Spirit would provide. Something He would pour out and that was the Spirit's Law, the Spirit's message, salvation and all of its equivalence . That is what that passage means. The idea of "all flesh", is just like the prophetic statement "all nations" in Isa. 2 and other places. It is just like Jesus saying go preach the gospel to "every creature". All flesh indicates not just the Jews but the Gentiles as well. In the statement "pour out His Spirit on all flesh", the Spirit is named for what the Spirit would do in this gospel age which Joel calls the "last days".

Chart #54

ACTS 2:21, 36-41

And it shall come to pass that whoever calls on the name of the Lord shall be saved.' **(cf.Rom 10:12-13)**

... 36 "Therefore let all the house of Israel know assuredly that God has made this Jesus, whom you crucified, both Lord and Christ." Now when they heard this, they were cut to the heart, and said to Peter and the rest of the apostles, "Men and brethren, what shall we do?" Then Peter said to them, "Repent, and let every one of you be baptized in the name of Jesus Christ for the remission of sins; and you shall receive the gift of the Holy Spirit. "For the promise is to you and to your children, and to all who are afar off, as many as the Lord our God will call." And with many other words he testified and exhorted them, saying, "Be saved from this perverse generation." Then those who gladly received his word were baptized; and that day about three thousand souls were added to them.

Day Of PENTECOST

I believe that is what the passage is talking about. In verse 21, the Apostle Peter quotes Joel 2:32; **"And it shall come to pass that whoever calls on the name of the Lord shall be saved."** I believe this is the text of Peters sermon because when he made that statement the question comes to mind "who is this Lord that I ought to call on and why should I do it and how do I go about it?". That is what Peter is going to tell us. Note that in the statement **"whoever calls on the name of the Lord shall be saved"**, the religious world in general seems only to see **"call on the name of the Lord"** and think it is talking about prayer. They miss the force of this statement entirely. This is another one of those statements that indicate that it is not just for the Jews. The emphasis is on the "whoever" . Whether the person is Jew or Gentile makes no difference, and I will show you, in just a minute, that this is the case. These things had to be pointed out because the Old Testament Law was a codified message to the Jews only. Now there is no distinction between them, both Jews and Gentiles are to receive this salvation that Peter (Joel) is talking about. Thus, the emphasis is on the "whoever" and the "calling on the name of the Lord" simply means to invoke His blessing (i.e. salvation) by doing what He says. Therefore, both Jew and Gentile have the right to invoke His blessing by doing what He says.

ROMANS 10:12-13

The Apostle Paul points out in Rom. 10:9-10 that faith in the Lord and confessing that faith is necessary to salvation: **"For with the heart one believeth unto righteousness, and with the mouth confession is made unto salvation."** Then he writes: **"For the Scripture says, "Whoever believeth on Him will not be put to shame. For there is no distinction between Jew and Greek, for the same Lord over all is rich to all who call upon Him. For "whoever calls upon the name of the Lord shall be saved."** So, the Apostle Paul points out that what Joel really was emphasizing was the fact that both Jew and Gentile would have the right to invoke God's blessing by doing what He says. Thus, the statement **"And it shall come to pass that whoever calls on the name of the Lord shall be saved."** is emphasizing both Jew and Gentile. Someone says "Well the Apostle Peter did not understand that". Sure he didn't understand it, like he didn't understand what he said in verse 39 either because it took a miracle to get him to go to those gentiles. But that is beside the point. In this instance, in quoting the prophecy of Joel and looking at the explanation of the inspired writer Paul it is unmistakable that the emphasis is on the "whoever", both Jew and Gentile.

With that in mind let's continue with our text in Acts 2. Peter said: **"Therefore let all the house of Israel know assuredly that God has made this Jesus, whom you crucified, both Lord and Christ. Now when they heard this, they were cut to the heart, and said to Peter and the rest of the apostles, "Men and brethren, what shall we do? Then Peter said to them, "Repent, and let every one of you be baptized in the name of Jesus Christ for the remission of sins; and you shall receive the gift of the Holy Spirit."** Let us suppose that the phrase **"for the remission of sins"** was not included in that text. Men have argued about this prepositional phase "unto the remission of sins" but look at the context. When these men asked the question "what shall we do" what information were they seeking? I understand the Greek and the grammatical construction but I do not believe I have to know that in order to know what they wanted to know and that they received that answer. They wanted to know what they needed to be saved, didn't they? Sure they did. Did Peter answer their question? Of course he did. What did he tell them to do? He said repent and be baptized. My point is that if the phrase "for the remission of sins" was not even in the text you would know and I would know what they needed to do was to repent and be baptized because he answered their question "what shall we do?" Do for what? Do in order to receive forgiveness of their sins. Then, he says, you shall receive the gift of the Holy Spirit. Why would they receive the gift?: **"For the promise is to you and to your children, and to all who are afar off, as many as the Lord our God will call."** What promise? The promise in the text of his sermon (v21) that "whoever shall call on the name of the Lord shall be saved". Let me show you why that it is: **"The promise is to you"** is talking about the Jews because that was the make up of the audience **"and to your children",** still talking about the Jews **"and to all who are afar off",** now he is talking about the Gentiles. Just as verse 21 is talking about the Jew and Gentile, so is this because he said "whoever" and that is talking about both Jew and Gentile. So, Peter is saying the promise is to you (Jews) and your children (Jewish offspring) and to the Gentiles who are afar off. Thus, the promise of verse 39 has to do with the promise of salvation involved in this text. You will receive what the Holy Spirit promised and what He promised was that **"whoever calls on the name of the Lord shall be saved".** So, I submit to you that the "gift of the Holy Spirit " is included in the promise prophesied by Joel and quoted by Peter. Thus, the Holy Spirit would give them salvation. Someone may say, "Now wait a minute preacher, you are being redundant, you are saying the same thing. You are having Peter say repent and be baptized and receive the remission of sins and I will give you remission of your sins". But consider this; sometimes salvation is made equal with the remission of sins, I know that, and sometimes they are used interchangeably, but not always. In Lk. 1:77 we have the prophecy of Zechariah (and I will start at verse 67 to get the whole prophecy): **"Now his father Zacharias was filled with the Holy Spirit, and prophesied, saying: Blessed is the Lord God of Israel, for He has visited and redeemed His people, and has raised up a horn of salvation for us in the house of His servant David, as He spoke by the mouth of His holy prophets, who have been since**

the world began, that we should be saved from our enemies and from the hand of all who hate us, to perform the mercy promised to our fathers and to remember His holy covenant, the oath which He swore to our father Abraham: to grant us that we, Being delivered from the hand of our enemies, might serve Him without fear, in holiness and righteousness before Him all the days of our life. and you, child, will be called the prophet of the Highest; for you will go before the face of the Lord to prepare His ways," Now, in verse 77 we have the statement of particular interest to us: **"to give knowledge of salvation to His people by the remission of their sins,"** Obviously, he uses salvation here to indicate a state or condition that would not exist had they not received remission of sins. So, there is a present salvation to the child of God and that is what this passage says. So, I submit to you that it is not redundant to say in Acts 2:38 that Peter promised them that if they would repent and be baptized they would receive remission of sins and they would also receive what the Holy Spirit promised.

Now, let's continue to look at the remote context of Peter's sermon. In Gal. 3:13-14, Paul writes: **"Christ has redeemed us from the curse of the law, having become a curse for us (for it is written, "Cursed is everyone who hangs on a tree"), that the blessing of Abraham might come upon the Gentiles in Christ Jesus, that we might receive the promise of the Spirit through faith."**

Chart #55
PROMISE OF THE SPIRIT--GAL 3:14
1. Made to Abraham (3:7-9) 2. Inspired promise (Gen. 28:8; 13:15; 17:18) 3. Included Gentiles (3:14). 4. The blessing of Abraham in Christ received (3:14) 5. Said to be the promise of the spirit-- the promise by faith (3:22) **Note:** They received what the spirit promised -- not the spirit himself!
THIS BLESSING = GIFT OF THE HOLY SPIRIT

So, we have the expression "received the promise of the Spirit through faith". In verse 8 we have the expression of the promise to Abraham ,"In you all the nations shall be blessed." Now, what does the "all the nations" include? It included both Jews and Gentiles just like it did in Isa. 2; in Mic. 2; in Mat. 28 ; in Mk. 16 and in Joel 2. So, this idea of promise of the Spirit through faith implies that it would come upon the Gentiles. What was the promise made to Abraham? Well, you know what it was; "In you all nations shall be blessed". Paul said that Abraham preached the gospel in promise. So, this was an inspired promise that we read about in Gen. 12:8; 13:15; 17:8. What does Paul mean by "promise of the Spirit"? It was an inspired promise made to Abraham and it included the Gentiles; verse 14:**"that the blessing of Abraham might come upon the Gentiles in Christ Jesus, that we might receive the promise of the Spirit through faith."** So, this is a commentary on Acts 2:38, they received what the Spirit promised, not the Spirit Himself but the blessing, the Gift of the Holy Spirit, and what they received here was that gift of the Holy Spirit. The blessing that came through Abraham, through Christ in His death, can rightfully be said to be that which the Holy Spirit promised. Why can not that same thing be called the gift? I believe that it is precisely that.

Acts 26:15-18 I believe is a parallel passage and also a commentary on our subject. Jesus appeared unto Saul on his way to Damascus and Paul is relating that event: **"So I said, 'Who are You, Lord?' And He said, 'I am Jesus, whom you are persecuting. But rise and stand on your feet; for I have appeared to you for this purpose, to make you a minister and a witness both of the things which you have seen and of the things which I will yet reveal to you. I will deliver you from the Jewish people, as well as from the Gentiles, to whom I now send you, to open their eyes and to turn them from darkness to light, and from the power of Satan to God, that they may receive forgiveness of sins and an inheritance among those who are sanctified by faith in Me.'** " That passage is parallel to the passage in Acts 2:38. Remission of sins and an inheritance; that promised inheritance, salvation now and salvation hereafter. There are those who will tell you "There was one plan of salvation to the Jews and another one to the Gentiles" and they cite this passage trying to make a difference in it but you know that the plan is the same for both Jew and Gentile. Just like I know that Acts 3:19 is the same where Peter said: "**Repent therefore and be converted, that your sins may be blotted out, so that times of refreshing may come from the presence of the Lord,**" These are all comparable statements, all talking about the same redemptive plan for saving those who will obey God and His Law. Now the question is how? How can the gift of the Holy Spirit and the promise of the Holy Spirit in Gal. 3, be salvation and all of its equivalence? Let me lay some ground work for the point that I want to make on this.

FIRST PETER ON SALVATION

If you read the book of First Peter you find that there are a number of relationships that the writer describes. He talks about these people who had been redeemed by the blood of Jesus (1:9). He said that their souls had been purified (1:22); that they had been born again, not of corruptible seed but incorruptible by the word of the living God that lives and abides forever, (1:23). They were God's elect, (1:1); they had been sanctified, (1:2); they had a living hope, (1:3); they expected an inheritance that was incorruptible, undefiled, that would not fade away, (1:4). That, ladies and gentlemen is a commentary on eternal life, precisely, an inheritance that will not fade away reserved in heaven for you. He said they were guarded by God through faith, (1:5) and this was unto that inheritance that would not fade away. He said they were a holy and royal priesthood, (2:5-9), they were God's own possession, (2:9) and they had the promise of eternal glory, (5:10). Now, the Holy Spirit prophesied this salvation and the Holy Spirit announced this salvation. That is what Peter said about these people that we know to be Christians.

I want to go back to 1:6 and begin reading this statement by Peter: "**In this you greatly rejoice, though now for a little while, if need be, you have been grieved by various trials, that the genuineness of your faith, being much more precious than gold that perishes, though it is tested by fire, may be found to praise, honor, and glory at the revelation of Jesus Christ, whom having not seen you love. Though now you do not see Him, yet believing, you rejoice with joy**

inexpressible and full of glory, do receiving the end of your faith--the salvation of your souls."

Chart #56
I Pet. 1:10-12 --ON SALVATION
1) REDEEMED BY THE BLOOD OF JESUS (1:9); 2) SOULS PURIFIED (1:22); 3) BEEN BORN AGAIN (1:23); 4) GOD'S ELECT (1:1); 5) BEEN SANCTIFIED (1:2); 6) HAD A LIVING HOPE (1:3); 7) EXPECTED AN INHERITANCE THAT WAS INCORRUPTIBLE, UNDEFILED, THAT WOULD NOT FADE AWAY (1:4) 8) GUARDED BY GOD THROUGH FAITH (1:5); 9) HOLY & ROYAL PRIESTHOOD (2:5,9); 10) 10) GOD'S OWN POSSESSION (2:9) 11) PROMISE OF ETERNAL GLORY (5:10) THE HOLY SPIRIT **PROPHESIED** THIS SALVATION THE HOLY SPIRIT **ANNOUNCED** THIS SALVATION THE HOLY SPIRIT **REVEALED** THIS SALVATION
DESCRIBING THE GIFT OF THE HOLY SPIRIT

Receiving the end of your faith, the salvation of your souls. Peter said these people had salvation. Look at verse 10, concerning which salvation the prophets searched and sought diligently, who prophesied of the grace that would come to you. That is why I include the statements at the end of my Chart, they prophesied and announced. They prophesied as the Spirit gave them utterance, II Pet. 1: 20. So he said in verse 11: **"searching what, or what manner of time, the Spirit of Christ who was in them was indicating when He testified beforehand the sufferings of Christ and the glories that would follow."** That is a statement that literally means the Spirit that testified of the Christ. It is what is called an elliptical statement because the Spirit by these prophets testified of the coming of the Christ. And this is what the statement means and so he continues to say, verse 12: **"To them it was revealed that, not to themselves, but to us they were ministering the things which now have been reported to you through those who**

have preached the gospel to you by the Holy Spirit sent from heaven-- things which angels desire to look into." What is he talking about when he said "receiving the end of your faith, the salvation of your souls"? He is simply indicating that the end result of their faith in Christ is the salvation that was promised to those who received the gospel preached to them by the inspiration of the Holy Spirit. Again, it is the Spirit that gave the message, it is His gift, the gift that He promised through the prophets.

This is how I can tell you that the bible indicates that the gift of the Holy Spirit can be, and is, salvation. That is, any and all blessing in Christ. If you identify some blessing that one has in Christ then it is included in that "gift of the Holy Spirit" of Acts 2:38. Peter is, clearly, talking about what God would provide for man in this age, the last days because that is what Joel prophesied and Peter calls our attention to it. This salvation was predicted in prophecy through the gospel by the Holy Spirit. This salvation was revealed and offered through the gospel by the Holy Spirit, (1Pet. 1:12). It was confirmed and verified by the Holy Spirit, (Heb. 2:1-4): **"Therefore we must give the more earnest heed to the things we have heard, lest we drift away. For if the word spoken through angels proved steadfast, and every transgression and disobedience received a just reward, how shall we escape if we neglect so great a salvation, which at the first began to be spoken by the Lord, and was confirmed to us by those who heard Him, God also bearing witness both with signs and wonders, with various miracles, and gifts of the Holy Spirit, according to His own will?"**

So, there are three things about the salvation you enjoy in this life as a child of God that involved the Holy Spirit. It was predicted in prophecy; it was revealed and offered through the gospel; it was confirmed and verified by the Holy Spirit. That is the gift of the Holy Spirit ladies and gentlemen. I do not have any doubt about it and I believe that is precisely what the passages that we compared indicate. I hope that you don't ask me what is the gift of the Holy Spirit after this lesson is over.

Chart #57
GIFT OF THE HOLY SPIRIT
HOW? ... can the "gift of the Holy Spirit"be salvation: Any & all blessings in Christ?
1. This salvation was predicted in prophecy through the gospel by the Holy Spirit-- 1 Peter 1:10 2. This salvation was revealed & offered through the gospel by the Holy Spirit - -1 Peter 1:12 3. This salvation was confirmed & verified by the Holy Spirit - - Hebrews 2:1-4 **-- SALVATION –** **PROPHESIED / REVEALED / VERIFIED } By the Holy Spirit!**
PROMISED - REVEALED - VERIFIED

I believe there is salvation now in this life and there is a future salvation, (Rom. 13:11): **"And do this, knowing the time, that now it is high time to awake out of sleep; for now our salvation is nearer than when we first believed."** The Holy Spirit made it possible by announcing the gospel of Jesus Christ. With that in mind we will now turn our thoughts to the matter of the indwelling of the Holy Spirit.

HOW DOES THE SPIRIT INDWELL?

As I said to you earlier, I know that the Holy Spirit dwells in the Christian. I know that the Holy Spirit leads. I don't have any problem with that but the question is how does He do it. You would think that our brethren would give some serious thought to what they are saying when they claim the Holy Spirit dwells in their body. They will charge, "Well you don't believe in the Holy Spirit". I answer, "Yes I do! But look, does He dwell in your body or does He dwell in your life?" That is just like the way "gift of the Holy Spirit" is used by many; is He the gift or is He the giver? It is not something you can answer that simply.

Chart #58
" IN YOU" or **IN YOUR BODY OR LIFE: WHICH?**
1) THE HOLY SPIRIT IS IN THE CHRISTIAN --- (Rom 8:9) 2) GOD THE FATHER IS IN THE CHRISTIAN --- (I Jno. 4:15) 3) JESUS CHRIST IS IN THE CHRISTIAN --- (Jno. 14:20) **QUESTION:** Why Must the Holy Spirit Dwell Directly in the Body of the Christian, but the Father & Son Does Not?
- - IN ONE'S LIFE - - **NOT IN HIS BODY!**

When the bible talks about the Holy Spirit being in the child of God does that mean in his body? The Holy Spirit is a divine being and we studied that in the first lesson of this series. Remember that I said to you that when you take a position on the Holy Spirit, you should never lose sight of the fact that He is a being, an individual, a person, not an "it". Just as the Father is a person, just as the Son is a person so is the Holy Spirit a person and He is divine just as they are, (Acts 5). So, you need to stop and think about this before you decide that there is a divine being dwelling in your body. In Rom. 8:9, the Holy Spirit is said to be in the Christian: **"But you are not in the flesh but in the Spirit, if indeed the Spirit of God dwells in you. Now if anyone does not have the Spirit of Christ, he is not His."** I am not denying that He is but ladies and gentlemen, the Father is in the Christian,(I Jno. 4:15): **"Whoever confesses that Jesus is the Son of God, God abides in him, and he in God."** Paul, in Rom. 8:9, says you are not in the flesh but in the Spirit if indeed the Spirit of God dwell in you. So, you are in the Spirit and the Spirit is in you. But John says God abides in you and you abide in God. The same expression concerning the indwelling of God and of the Spirit. Also, notice that Jesus said, Jno. 14:20; "**At that day you will know that I am in My Father, and you in Me, and I in you.**" Now, tell me that these are not saying the same thing. So, my question is this: When it comes to the Holy Spirit, why must He dwell directly in my body but the Father and the Son do not? We understand that the Father and the Son are in our lives. Why then, must the Holy Spirit indwell the body? The exact same language is used in all three cases. They understand that when you have fellowship with the Father and the Son you are living the life they want you to live; they are in your life. Our brethren understand that, when it involves the Father and the Son. Why then do they not understand that to be the case when it involves the Holy Spirit? God is a comprehensive term. I am convinced that any time the term "God" appears in the bible, from the beginning of Genesis through Revelations, it always means the "Father, Son, and Holy Spirit", the Godhead, unless it is otherwise indicated either by way of the context or explicitly stated. It is that kind of term. Obviously, the term God in I Jno. 4 refers to the Father because the verse just before it talks about the Father and the Son. My question to them is this: "What do you have to say about this verse that states that God the Father is in the Christian?" Do you think they would say He is in our body? You know they will not claim that to be the case even though the language concerning indwelling is exactly the same for all three of the individuals of the Godhead. So the Holy Spirit is in my life not in my body. He had better be in my life and He had better be in your life in the same way that the Father and the Son are in our lives.

MIND CONTROL

Let's look at this passage in Eph. 3:15-17. What I am going to show you is mind control used by those who want you to believe that the Holy Spirit dwells in your body. I mentioned ,to you, the statement in Mat. 3 where John says that Jesus will baptize with the Holy Spirit and with fire. I pointed out that there are those who will say, "that is a promise to everybody". But I say to you "No, that tells you who will do the baptizing, it does not say who will receive it". Now look at this passage in Eph. 3 starting at verse 15: **"from whom the whole family in heaven and earth is named, that He would grant you, according to the riches of His glory, to be strengthened with might through His Spirit in the inner man, that Christ may dwell in your hearts through faith; that you, being rooted and grounded in love,".**

Chart #59

MIND CONTROL

Eph. 3:15-17

from whom the whole family in heaven and earth is named, that He would grant you, according to the riches of His glory, to be strengthened with might through His Spirit in the inner man, that Christ may dwell in your hearts through faith; that you, being rooted and grounded in love,

Col. 1:9-11

For this reason we also, since the day we heard it, do not cease to pray for you, and to ask that you may be filled with the knowledge of His will in all wisdom and spiritual understanding; that you may have a walk worthy of the Lord, fully pleasing Him, being fruit-ful in every good work and increasing in the knowledge of God; strengthened with all might, according to His glorious power, for all patience and longsuffering with joy;

By Charismatic Preachers

There are those who will say, "See there that says the Holy Spirit is in the inner man". I don't know whether you watch any of these religious programs on television or not but if you do you will see things like some great big muscular fellow taking a telephone book and rip it into and claim that the Holy Spirit enables him to do that. They do that because they claim the Holy Spirit is in their physical body when in reality is was exercise that made them strong. That passages doesn't say that the Spirit is in the inner man. That is what is called an "eye deceiver". That is not what the passage says; the strength is in the inner man, not the Spirit. How is it accomplished? It is accomplished by the Holy Spirit. So, he says strengthened with might by (or through) His Spirit. The strength is in the inner man not the outer man, not in the body.

The Apostle Paul wrote both of these books, Ephesians and Colossians, and Col. 1:9-11 is a companion passage to Eph. 3:15-17. It is quite often the case that whatever Paul discusses in one of these letters he also mentions in the other. So, it is always wise to check both letters when a text is being examined. He says; **"For this reason we also, since the**

day we heard it, do not cease to pray for you, and to ask that you may be filled with the knowledge of His will in all wisdom and spiritual understanding; that you may have a walk worthy of the Lord, fully pleasing Him, being fruitful in every good work and increasing in the knowledge of God; strengthened with all might, according to His glorious power, for all patience and longsuffering with joy;" How is the inner man strengthened? Paul says he is strengthened by a knowledge of His will, by the message that the Spirit has revealed. So, Paul is not talking about the strength in the body, he is talking about the strength of the inner man, made strong by a knowledge of the message written by the inspiration of the Spirit, the gospel of Christ.

FIRST CORINTHIANS 6:19

I must look at First Corinthians 6:19 and then I want to go back to Rom. 8 again to look at the contrast that Paul makes between the carnal and the spiritual man. Someone says, "Well preacher, you don't believe your bible because it says in 1Cor. 6 that the Spirit is in your body." Let's see if that is the case: **"Or do you not know that your body is the temple of the Holy Spirit who is in you, whom you have from God, and you are not your own? For you were bought at a price; therefore glorify God in your body and in your spirit, which are God's."** In this section of the letter to the Corinthians, Paul was talking to them, specifically, about sexual immorality. In verse 18 he said: **"Flee sexual immorality. Every sin that a man does is outside the body, but he who commits sexual immorality sins against his own body."** He is pointing out that the body of man is for something other than gratification; that the body ought to be use for something other than sexual gratification. He points out that prior to their conversion, these Corinthians did not know this. There was a problem in this church that they were faced with, a problem of sexual immorality. So, I need to understand that this is what he is talking about; he is talking about the fact that the body should be used for something other than just physical satisfaction. In view of that, he says "don't you know that your body is the temple of the Holy Spirit which is in you? " Again, that did not say that the Holy Spirit is in your body; that is not what it says. He said, "which you have from God" and now watch the next statement: "You were bought by a price, therefore glorify God in your body".

My question is this: How do I glorify God in my body? Do I glorify God by becoming muscular? Or, when I lose my hair, I put a wig on? Is that how I glorify Him? How do you glorify God with your body? You do it in the life that you live! So, they miss it again, don't they? That is how you glorify God. That is the very reason these fellows get on television ripping books apart, claiming the Holy Spirit has made them strong. No, that is not it at all and that is not what this passage says. Paul said glorify God therefore in your body. How do you glorify God in your body? You glorify God by the life you live ; By what you do! It is an easy thing to find a passage that has Spirit and body in it and completely ignore what precedes it and what follows it and come up with an erroneous conclusion. People who love the truth is not going to do that.

A CONTRAST IN WALK

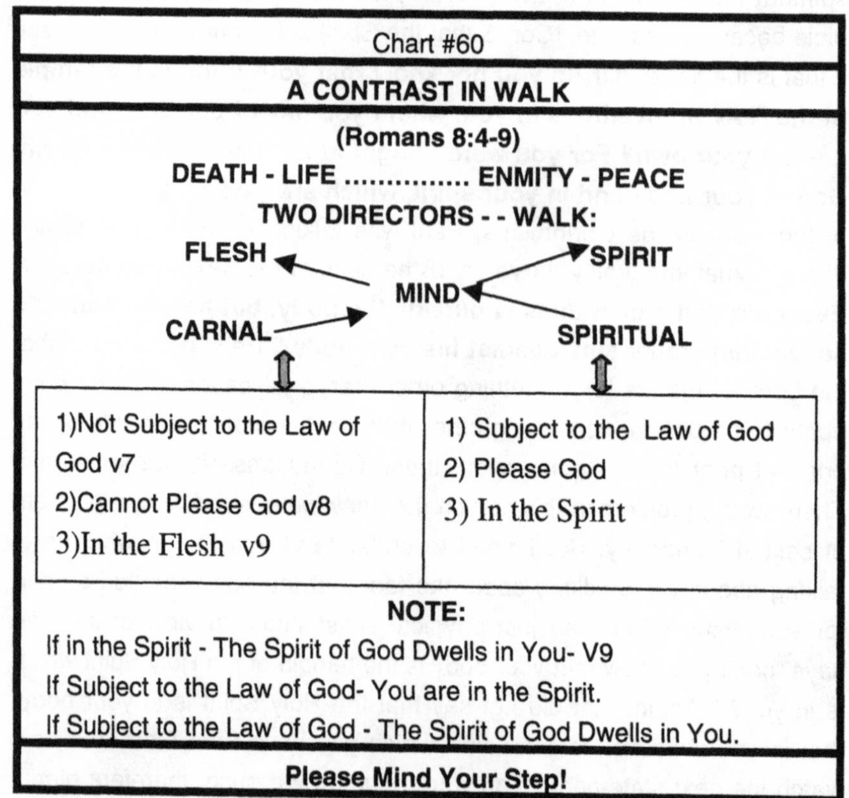
Chart #60

A CONTRAST IN WALK

(Romans 8:4-9)

1)Not Subject to the Law of God v7 2)Cannot Please God v8 3)In the Flesh v9	1) Subject to the Law of God 2) Please God 3) In the Spirit

NOTE:

If in the Spirit - The Spirit of God Dwells in You- V9

If Subject to the Law of God- You are in the Spirit.

If Subject to the Law of God - The Spirit of God Dwells in You.

Please Mind Your Step!

I will go over this quickly but I believe this is decisive of the issue of how the Spirit dwells in someone. Paul presents a contrast here in Rom. 8. He presents a contrast between **"walking after the flesh"** and **"walking after the spirit".** He has a man, not half of a man on one side and half of a man on the other, but a whole man who is being directed. His direction is either coming from the Spirit or is coming from the flesh. Paul says: **"that the righteous requirement of the law might be fulfilled in us who do not walk according to the flesh but according to the Spirit."** The implication is that this man walks according to the Spirit. According to I. G. Grubbs, in his booklet on hermeneutics," the exact extinct and limit of a contrast is established by the contrast itself". So, Paul is talking about two directives. Thus, the word "walk" is implied in the phrase "according to the Spirit". Then he tells us what those who walk after the flesh are doing: **"For those who live according to the flesh set their minds on the things of the flesh, but those who live according to the Spirit, the things of the Spirit."** The contrast has been set and the phrases that follow, though not stated fully, are all talking about this same contrast, that of the spirit versus the flesh. Not only are we told by Grubbs that this is the case but the law of language demands this of a contrast as well. I have been told by English Teachers that this is so.

They that walk after the flesh mind the things of the flesh, they do what they want to do and not what God has directed. However, those that walk after the Spirit minds the things of the Spirit by doing what the Spirit wants them to do and that is what the passage says. Then Paul says: **"For to be carnally minded is death, but to be spiritually minded is life and peace."** Those that mind the things of the flesh have death but those that mind the things of the Spirit has the opposite, they have life and peace. Then he adds to this the idea of the mind of the flesh being enmity against God. Those that are walking after flesh are the same as those that are carnal minded. You cannot help but see the contrast there. You need only to look at the opposites to see that. One is enmity against God and will produce death because that person is not in the right relationship with God. The other is life and peace. Do you know that the word peace means, literally, a right relationship? Enmity is the exact opposite of peace. In the New Testament, peace means "right relationship" and is used to refer to the relationship of man with God; the relationship of man with wife; the relationship of Jew with Gentile, the right relationship of man with his fellow man. So, here is a fellow who has the right relationship with God and has peace; he is walking after the Spirit, and another one who does not have a right relationship but enmity with God; he is walking after the flesh. Now Paul will focus in on that man who walks after the flesh. He will tell us what his big problem is for he says: **"Because the carnal mind is enmity against God; for it is not subject to the law of God, nor indeed can be."** He is insubordinate to the law of God. The word "subject" means subordinate; the opposite is insubordinate. So, this fellow who is walking after the flesh is insubordinate to God's law.

I want to ask everybody here a question: If these are opposites, and they are, what is the man doing that is walking after the Spirit while his opposite is being insubordinate to the law of God? Obviously, he is subordinate to the law of God. The man walking after the flesh is not subject, the man walking after the Spirit is subject to the Law of God. The one that is not subject is insubordinate the man walking after the Spirit is subordinate. That is what Paul says. He makes that distinction between those of a carnal mind and those that are spiritual minded . He starts this discussion out in verse 2: **"For the law of the Spirit of life in Christ Jesus has made me free from the law of sin and death. So then, those who are in the flesh cannot please God."** It follows then that the one walking after the Spirit is subject to the law of God, he is doing what God wants him to do. Paul said: **"But you are not in the flesh but in the Spirit, if indeed the Spirit of God dwells in you. Now if anyone does not have the Spirit of Christ, he is not His."** This fellow who is in the flesh is doing the things of the flesh, he is walking after the flesh; the contrast demands it. If I just look at the statement "in the flesh" and decided that it means anybody who is alive, (there are those who have done that), then I do not get the force of the contrast. The man that is walking after the Spirit is also alive and so that is not what he is talking about. You have to look at the context of the contrast . He said you are not in the flesh; you are not walking after the flesh but after the Spirit if so be the Spirit of God dwells in you. Obviously, when the person is doing the will of God, walking after the things of the Spirit, then the Spirit of

God dwells in him. That is what this passage says. That is the only way that He dwells in you. Look at the formulated illustration of the Chart:

CARNAL MINDED	SPIRITUAL MINDED
Not subject to the Law of God v7	Subject to the Law of God
Cannot please God v 8	Pleases God
In the flesh v9	In the Spirit

NOTE: If in the Spirit , then the Spirit of God dwells in you. If subject to the Law of God, then you are in the Spirit. If subject to the Law of God, the spirit of God dwells in you. So, I submit to you that if one is subject to the Law of God, the Spirit dwells in him and that is the only way that the Spirit indwells the Christian. When he allows the Spirit's law to be in his heart directing his thinking and his life, then the Spirit dwells in him.

"LED BY THE SPIRIT"

I believe that Rom. 8:14 is decisive of the issue of being led by the Spirit just as the chapter is decisive of the issue of indwelling as we have already noted. Paul says: **"For as many as are led by the Spirit of God, these are sons of God."**

Chart #61
"LED BY THE SPIRIT"
(Rom. 8:14) **- - Not Dragged - -** 1. THE SPIRIT'S LAW GIVES DIRECTIONS (V 2) 2. THE SPIRITUALLY MINDED SUBMIT (V 5) 3. ALL WHO DO SO ARE LED BY THE SPIRIT. **NOTE: "AS MANY AS..."**

Question: What does "as many as" suggest to your mind? It should suggest the idea of "no more and no less". This verse is just past where we were reading concerning the contrast of "flesh" and "spirit" and where

I suggested to you that the Spirit dwells in you when you let the Spirit's Law guide your life. Now what does in mean to be "led by the Spirit"? The person is not being dragged by the Spirit or forced to do anything against his own will. It is not that at all. Rather, it is as follows: 1. The Spirit's law gives direction, verse 2; 2. The Spiritually minded submits to His will, verse 5; 3. All who do so are led by the Spirit, verse 14. Sons of God are those walking after the things of the Spirit, not just some but all (as many as) that are in subjection to the Law of God.

Now let's look at verses 26 and 27, in context, and see if we can determine what Paul is talking about when he says: **"Likewise the Spirit also helps in our weaknesses. For we do not know what we should pray for as we ought, but the Spirit Himself makes intercession for us with groanings which cannot be uttered. Now He who searches the hearts knows what the mind of the Spirit is, because He makes intercession for the saints according to the will of God."** Invariably, when I discuss this subject I am asked about this particular passage. That is why I decided to include this passage in this particular lesson. Note the beginning of verse 26 where he says "likewise"(NKJ) or in like manner(ASV) . Brethren, when you are reading along and come to a term such as "likewise" or its equivalent, what does that suggest to your mind? This term is indicative of a conclusion being drawn from the preceding statements. He has been talking about something just prior to this that has some kind of bearing on it. He had been talking about the matter of suffering in verse 17 and he pointed out that in suffering trials and tribulations, the Christians hope will help him. You know that; Heb. 6:17-19 as we discussed before tells us the same thing. Now he says here is something else that will help him.

The question is often asked, is Paul talking about the Holy Spirit or is he talking about the human spirit? Brethren, no one has ever successive accused me of straddling the fence on anything. But in this instance, I think Paul is speaking of both, certainly it is the human spirit and I am going to show you why I know that. It is the human spirit that has been enlightened by the Holy Spirit so both are involved. Let me present some information for your consideration. Paul had been talking about the creation suffering and, whatever it may be worth to you, I do not believe he is talking about the whole creation including crabgrass and fire ants and things of that nature. That does not make sense. He is talking about somebody that waits for the revealing of the Sons of God. So, the term creature or creation is used to indicate a New Creature in Christ and that is the Christian, (Rom. 6:3-5).

He goes on and talks about the "first fruits", a reference to the apostles, and says they were not being exempt. If "any man" is in Christ he is going to suffer persecution,(II Tim. 3:12): **"Yes, and all who desire to live godly in Christ Jesus will suffer persecution."**

CHART #62

ROMANS 8:26-27

- - IN CONTEXT - -

ROM. 8:18-25 - - "SUFFERING" (V18; Cf. V17)

1) Vs. 19-22 - - CREATION/NEW CREATURE in Christ (Rom. 6:3-5)
2) V. 23 - - 1st - FRUITS/APOSTLES

} Both are said to "Groan"

ROM. 8:24-25 - - HOPE HELPS (Heb 6:17-19)
ROM. 8:26-27 - - "IN LIKE MANNER..."
Like Manner –means Something Else
Something Else Helps
Still the Same Ones "Groaning"

NOTE: THE GROANING IS BY THE ONE WHO IS
1) SUFFERING
2) PRAYING

NOTE: HEART-SEARCHER KNOWS THE MIND OF THE SUFFERING ONE WHO IS PRAYING

"WE KNOW NOT HOW TO PRAY AS WE OUGHT"

So, Paul is talking about trials and tribulations and he points out that hope helps us in this matter. He is talking about those who suffer persecution and he said hope helps, i.e. the hope they have in Christ Jesus. Then he said "likewise" here is something else that helps. The "something else" means in addition to, and that the something else helps. Note that in both places they are groaning (verses 22-23 and 27). The ones groaning in verse 22 are the same ones groaning here in verse 27. The groaning is by the one that is suffering and the one that is praying. That much is evident, there is not any question about it. The heart searcher knows the mind of the suffering one who is praying. That much, I think is simple, I can see that. That is exactly what Paul is saying. These same people are groaning, they are being faced with the same problems. The "likewise" ties these passages together.

ROMANS 8:26

Question: Is this talking about the Holy Spirit groaning? Groaning indicates pain; does the Holy Spirit feel pain? How can you apply that to the Holy Spirit? Whoever this passage is talking about is groaning. Not only that but he says God knows the mind of the Spirit. He has no point if this is the Holy Spirit. Surely God knows His own Spirit. The Holy Spirit is certainly involved in this but that is not what he is talking about in this particular text. I talked to you, briefly, about equivocation. That is whenever a speaker or writer uses a term in one sense and in the next breath he uses it in a different sense without an indication that he has changed its meaning. To do that is just not right. I submit to you then that the "mind of the Spirit" in verse 27 is the "mind of the Spirit" in verse 6. That is the same fellow Paul is talking about. He is talking about the spiritual minded who: 1) Walk after the Spirit, v4; 2) Mind the things of the Spirit, v5; 3) By the Spirit puts to death the deeds of the body, v13; 4) Are led by the Spirit, v14; 5) Are subject to the Law of God, v7; 6) In whom the Spirit indwells, v9. God knows what is in the heart of man. Here is the intercession or the meeting with the Child of God and the "Heartsearcher",(v27). You could ask me forty questions that I could not and would not try to answer but I believe this is what Paul is teaching in Rom. 8. He is talking about those that are suffering, the ones that are groaning in their suffering and he simply says that in the presence of these tribulations you may not know what to ask but the heart searcher knows.

Let me give you a thought along these lines. You remember in Jam. 1 where James is talking about suffering. He addresses this suffering that we are talking about , he says, (Jam. 1:2ff): **"My brethren, count it all joy when you fall into various trials, knowing that the testing of your faith produces patience. But let patience have its perfect work, that you may be perfect and complete, lacking nothing."**

Chart #63

- - ROMANS 8:26 - -

SPIRIT & INTERCESSION

QUESTION: IS THIS THE HOLY SPIRIT?

1) GROANINGS - - Indicating PAIN

2) God Knows "What is the Mind of the Spirit" - - Has No Point (Surely God Knows His Own Spirit)

NOTE: "SPIRIT" (V. 26) IS THE SAME AS:

"Mind of the Spirit" (V. 27)

"Mind of the Spirit" (V. 6)

THE SPIRITUALLY MINDED WHO:

1) Walk After the Spirit (V. 4)
2) Mind the Things of the Spirit (V. 5)
3) By the Spirit Put to Death the Deeds of the Body (V 13)
4) Are Led by the Spirit (V. 14)
5) Are Subject to the Law of God (V. 7)
6) Spirit Indwells (V. 9)

GOD KNOWS WHAT IS IN THE HEART:

HERE IS THE "INTERCESSION" - - "MEETING WITH"

" INTERCESSION" = "MEETING WITH"

Also, in Rom.5:2ff, Paul addressed this subject of suffering where he said: **"And not only that, but we also glory in tribulations, knowing that tribulation produces perseverance; and perseverance, character; and character, hope. Now hope does not disappoint,**

because the love of God has been poured out in our hearts by the Holy Spirit who was given to us." The point is, trials and tribulations has a purpose in the life of the Christian. God knows that we need some trials, some suffering and tribulations. We may not be able to recognize that but it does help by making us stronger and more fit for service to our God. It is kind of like these young boys going out for football. I well remember that I had not done any exercise during the off season and after one day of Spring training even my toe nails hurt. I hurt all over, every muscle hurt. There was a reason for the conditioning process imposed upon us by the coaching staff. It was for what would happen later on. That is the purpose of trials and tribulations. Paul is talking about that in Rom. 8.

Now let's go back to James where he says: **"If any of you lacks wisdom, let him ask of God, who gives to all liberally and without reproach, and it will be given to him."** So, he couples prayer with these trials that we have. He says ask God who gives to all liberally. I believe that is the point Paul is making in Rom. 8 as well. He is simply indicating that when I am faced with trials and tribulations and even in difficult situations (and I have been in those situations where I did not know what to pray) God knows what you have need of. Someone whose body is racked with pain and they have a terminal disease, what do we say, what do we ask for? We don't know what to pray but He who searches the heart knows the groaning that comes from our heart and is able to understand. God knows the mind of the spiritual minded man and will supply the words we cannot utter "for we know not how to pray as we ought", (v26).

SEALED WITH HOLY SPIRIT

I had mentioned the seal of the Holy Spirit to you earlier in this series and I want to look at this Chart briefly with you and that will conclude the lesson. All of this is related. I am certain that every one of you here in this audience is a Gentile. Not that there is any reflection on the Jews; it is not that at all.

In Eph.1:1, Paul addressed the saints that were at Ephesus and the faithful in Christ Jesus. In verses 3 through 10 he uses the pronouns "us", "we, and "our" referring to the saints and the faithful, both Jew and